WHERE HAVE ALL THE JOBS GONE?

WHY AMERICANS ARE OUT OF WORK

BY
GEORGE VARGISH

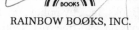

RAINBOW BOOKS, INC.

Library of Congress Cataloging-in-Publication Data

Vargish, George
    Where have all the jobs gone? : why Americans are out of work /
George Vargish.
        p. cm.
    Includes index.
    ISBN 0-935834-85-0 : $14.95
    1. Labor market--United States. 2. United States--Foreign
economic relations. 3. Offshore assembly industry--United States.
4. Manpower policy--United States. 5. Unemployment--United States.
I. Title.
HD5724.V37 1992
331.12'0973--dc20   92-22608
                                                              CIP

Where Have All The Jobs Gone?
Why Americans Are Out of Work
by George Vargish
Interior Design by Marilyn Ratzlaff
Cover Design by Therese Cabell
$14.95

Recognizing the importance of preserving the written word,
Rainbow Books, Inc., by policy, prints all of its first
editions on acid-free (pH Neutral) paper.

DEDICATION

To Emmaline

Other books by George Vargish:

What's Made In The U.S.A.?

Rutgers University, Transaction Books

1988

CONTENTS

ACKNOWLEDGMENTS

Grateful acknowledgment is made to the following for permission to reprint previously published material:

Politics Of The Rich And Poor by Kevin Phillips, excerpts. Published by Random House. Copyrighted 1988, 1990 by Random House. Permission granted by Random House.

The New York Times, Copyright 1990, 1991, 1992. Excerpts from articles: April 9, 1990, and December 16, 1990, by Louis Uchitelle; March 19, 1991, by Elizabeth M. Fowler; September 4, 1991, by Steven Greenhouse; January 1, 1992, by Andrew Pollack; February 18, 1992, by Clyde H. Farnsworth. Reprinted by permission of *The New York Times*.

The Next Century by David Halberstam, excerpts. Copyrighted 1991. Published by William Morrow and Company. Permission granted by William Morrow and Company.

The Rise And Fall Of The Great Powers by Paul Kennedy, excerpts. Published by Random House. Copyrighted 1988, 1990 by Random House. Permis-

INTRODUCTION

The so-called golden 1980s turned out to be an unrewarding time for most Americans. This *Teflon* period with its wild excesses in the financial sector, low morality in government, the alarming decline of our industrial sector, and the growing ranks of the poor in America prompted me to write *Where Have All The Jobs Gone?*

For most Americans, having a well-paying job meant economic health, a feeling of self-worth, and the possible means to achieve those dreams for a better life.

The inability of our government to feel any compassion for our people and to prepare our nation for the global economic war raging around us convinced me, and others like myself who spent a lifetime "in the trenches," that it was vital to focus on the source of our industrial decay and the need for decisive action to halt our descent into a third world economic status.

It is my hope that my book can arouse public opinion to compel our leaders to live by their elective responsibility and respond to the needs of our citizens rather than to continue in their same pattern of self-service.

If we act quickly, there is hope for America to revitalize our "job engines" to provide better-paying jobs for our citizens in all walks of life.

This book owes much to faithful supporters. George Cooke was my able literary consultant and critic. Seth M. Bodner briefed me on International Trade events. My son-in-law, James R. Redeker, supplied the legal expertise. Betty Wright, my publisher, and her staff provided professional guidance on many issues.

Finally, my associate and dedicated wife, Emmaline, toiled many days, researching, editing, counseling, and encouraging me to bring this report to a conclusion.

To all the above, and those not mentioned,

Thanks!

George Vargish
Saddle River, NJ

WHY AM I WORKING HARDER
AND EARNING LESS?

Most Americans still manage to find jobs. But for the vast majority, the standard of living is dropping steadily. This is in sharp contrast with the glowing reports emanating from Washington, D.C. of the "great prosperity" and the greatest economic growth in our history during the 1980s.

Politicians juggle statistics to justify their achievements on behalf of their constituents, but the numbers reported by the U.S. Bureau of Labor Statistics tell a different story. The average American now earns fewer net dollars than he did during the 1970s after inflation is factored in.

In his book *The Politics Of The Rich And Poor* (Random House), Kevin Phillips, advisor to Republican presidents and a leading political authority, writes of the great disparity in incomes that evolved in America during the so-called "great job expansion years" of the '80s. The top 20 percent of our working force experienced substantial increase in incomes, but the remainder saw a decline in net earnings.

Today's job seekers come from diverse backgrounds. They include college graduates, executives, managers, clerks, bookkeepers, mechanics, all types of skilled factory workers, the unskilled, and newly arrived immigrants. When they turn to the job market, what do they find?

"U.S. WAGES NOT GETTING AHEAD? BETTER GET USED TO IT?"

"For a brief moment in the mid-1980s, it looked as if Americans would again know how it feels to get ahead. Wages and family incomes seemed to be rising by just enough to promise more prosperous lives . . .

"Instead of continuing to rise, real incomes — that is, wages and salaries adjusted for inflation — have declined over the last three years . . .

" . . . The upshot is that most Americans are entering the 1990s worse off than they were in the early 1970s . . ."

(The New York Times, Sunday, December 16, 1990)

We are a work-oriented society. We believe that we can achieve the good life through work. Americans have always had high expectations. We saw our parents "off to work" and were exposed to their experiences in the process. We also learned that having a job gives us personal gratification. Having a job means that someone needs us, and work gives us an opportunity to exercise our skills.

Work also meets the obvious economic needs of the family. If you want "bread on the table" — get a job. Or if you want some of the material things in life and you come from an average American family — get a job! Having a job is the means of buying a new car, clothes, TV, travel and vacations, getting married, buying a home, or fulfilling a retirement dream.

Today, Americans are learning to expect less, to value themselves and others less. As the American dream fades away, the young pin their hopes on winning the state lottery or forget their anxieties with the help of drugs. Some turn to crime and violence. Pride in work is diminishing. Many workers are only marking time until they become eligible for pensions. What an incredible and sad shift in the American work ethic. With loss of hope, this new attitude of listlessness and indifference has crept over a large segment of our population.

How To Match Your Qualifications With The Market Needs

The college graduate, having prepared himself for "that day," looks forward with a mixture of excitement and fear to his first encounter with the job market-place. If he followed the usual pattern of part-time work when at school, he knows something about what it is like to have a job. Students tend to believe that when they have at last received that hard-earned degree, the world will be at their disposal. When they discover that no one wants them, that there are no jobs in their field, it can shatter their dreams and assumptions.

"STUDENTS FIND JOB SEARCH MUCH HARDER" (INCLUDED IN THIS JOB SEARCH ARE M.B.A. STUDENTS, GRADUATE ENGINEERS AND COMPUTER-TRAINED GRADUATES)

". . . Corporate recruiting on most campuses is way down, according to Richard J. Lewis, dean of both the College of Business and Graduate School of Business Administration at Michigan State University . . .

". . . The best students can probably find jobs . . . but may have to work harder to start their careers . . . . What advice would he give himself if he was a senior — not receiving job offers? — I would offer my services

free to gain the needed experience . . ."
(The New York Times, March 19, 1991).

After one of my lectures on economics and trade at Rider College in New Jersey, some of the students raised the question: What became of all the jobs that seemed to be "out there" when they started school? Although I had just finished a lecture on my theories for the declining job market, I could not temper the shock they were experiencing on a personal level as reality collided with their long-cherished dreams.

Once while visiting my grandson Brian, a senior at Villanova University, he asked with some concern where the jobs were. Brian indicated the graduating class was, on the whole, unsuccessful in finding employment and many students planned to go on for their M.B.A. degrees.

"What will happen when all these fellows go into the market for jobs?" asked Brian worriedly.

I offered what I hope was reassurance, but I am as concerned as Brian, and I have no job worries because I am retired.

A few years ago, the Ford Motor Company closed down an auto assembly plant in the town of Mahwah, New Jersey. Thousands of workers and supervisors were affected by this shut-down. According to press reports, the production workers experienced severe economic dislocations in trying to find new jobs offering the same wages at Ford. Many ended up with jobs paying half what they had earned at Ford. A sharp decline in living standards occurred, and with it a loss of faith in the American dream.

Another by-product of reduced income is severe family stress. Many divorces, separations, and in some cases suicide — can be traced to declining incomes and loss of hope.

New Jersey has seen a steady decline in manufacturing as its source of higher paying jobs. In the 1970s, manufacturing accounted for 40 percent of jobs, and today, only 18 percent. This general picture is true of the nation as a whole. So the former Ford assembly plant worker whose skills were centered in manufacturing settles for a job in the service area where pay is barely above the minimum wage and the future bleak.

The decline in the manufacturing has contributed considerably to the decay in our urban areas. For the first time in memory, a city in Connecticut declared bankruptcy. The mayor explained that with the departure of manufacturing jobs, unemployment was high, tax revenues did not meet municipal needs, and the local government could not meet its obligations. This bankruptcy shocked the area, but it is symptomatic of the economic disease spreading across our nation.

The unemployment statistics do not reflect the vast numbers of our youth who cannot find jobs and who resort to drugs and other forms of violence. The poor, with limited education and few skills, have no cause to believe "in the American dream" our forefathers had. What future is there in working in a fast-food place, washing windows, cutting grass, working in a retail establishment, or as a clerk in a bank?

Mergers, Transfers, Leveraged Buyouts, Job-Cuts, And Plant Shutdowns Take Their Toll Of White-Collar Americans

Public librarians have begun to report hordes of job seekers coming in to seek help in job prospecting. Libraries are stepping up the establishment of "career centers" to help these distressed individuals, many of whom are well-educated and middle-aged, unemployed for the first time in long careers.

Many executives, after adjusting painfully to new positions with less pay, feel insecure. Having lost their old seniority, they fear any additional personnel down-sizing in their new jobs will surely affect them.

It is a demoralizing experience to face the prospect of job-hunting again. The deep recession has created unemployment among white-collar workers at a level not seen since the Great Depression. Unfortunately, corporate America is obsessed with job-cutting, paying scant heed to their future needs.

The loss of a job, psychiatrists state, ranks behind the death of a loved one emotionally. Erosion of self-esteem sets in particularly if a new job is not forth–coming soon. The forecast is that one-third of American companies will reduce executive ranks annually for the next five years. Many executives face the prospect of rebuilding their lives after spending many years working for the same company. For many, pay cuts and the resultant down-scaling of their style of living affects the entire family, attitudes as well as allowances. State colleges are currently experiencing an avalanche of applications as the formerly affluent search for what is perhaps affordable.

Many of our citizens across the country are facing more than just the trauma of losing a job and finding another. They are unable to find any new job at all and are faced with the ordeal of finding some income to survive. The news media reported such a condition in Taylor County, Idaho, when the good jobs disappeared altogether. One-third of the farmers became the working poor with an annual income of about $6,000 per household. Those who work in subsistence jobs often become trapped in permanent poverty. They fall through the safety net of government aid due to regulations that forbid aid if two members of the family work. Two family members working to help the family survive has, however, become the rule and not the exception.

Bill Moyers produced a program that displayed in a graphic manner two wars — the winning of the Gulf War and the ongoing war involving our citizens in America to survive economically. The people interviewed in Bill Moyers' program suffered a common anguish — no jobs and a desperate search to find employment. The threat of losing a home, having no money for food or the bare necessities of life, and being forced to seek welfare aid is a burden too heavy for many families to bear. This gripping program was aired on public television on May 29, 1990.

The homeless people interviewed stated plainly they needed jobs, but there were none available. It is estimated that there are now one million homeless living on our streets.

The Moyers' program demonstrated the strong leadership and dedication of our government leaders to bring the Gulf War to a conclusion. The stark contrast lay in the obvious inability of our government to face up to the task of fashioning domestic programs to meet the needs of our citizens.

It is ironical to read of new service industries setting up shop to counsel the unemployed how to fill out resumes and seek employment. *All for a fee.*

Bad News For Hi-Tech And Management Employees

Citicorp of New York, the nation's largest bank, recently announced it was cutting back 17,000 jobs — mainly management and supporting staff members. Citicorp indicated that a weak economy and an uncertain banking environment was forcing this action. It is to be noted that under our policies foreigners can establish financial facilities in America with little resistance from our government. Try doing so in Japan!

It Is Estimated That 20 Percent Of
U.S. Banks Are Under Foreign Control

Digital Equipment Corporation of Maynard, Massachusetts, laid off 800 more workers according to a recent article in the press. This brings the layoffs to a total of 10,000 for the past year and a half. So hi-tech workers are now casting about to find new jobs. The New England region has experienced a deep recession for an extended period of time with reduced business in the hi-tech area which was a strong element in the economy of that region. The Far East led by Japan is moving freely into our computer business and other exotic areas of our market.

Does Washington Care?

I am an active member of the Service Corps of Retired Executives. I have learned that many clients formerly in executive positions seek counseling to establish their own businesses. Unfortunately, the decision to go into business very often springs out of fear and desperation to provide for loved ones.

The following chart tells the story.

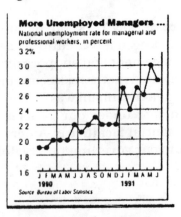

Permanent Part-time Workers
Mean Permanent Poverty

Retailers and other businesses have turned to hiring part-time workers. Some workers are "permanent part-time" employees. The advantage is that these employees may be excluded from health insurance, pension, sick leave, and paid vacations. They have many other disadvantages. Their work schedules are at the whim of the employer, presenting a strain on the employee, particularly if children are involved.

Many of these workers are *involuntary* part-timers. They are paid near the minimum wage in many cases and must seek more than one job to stay near the poverty level. As a government statistic, a part-time worker is considered a full-timer despite their small earnings, lack of benefits, and undesirable working conditions.

Desperate for work, the part-timer has no alternative but to accept substandard conditions in order to survive. This job category is growing rapidly and is far more common than people realize.

A Legislator Acts

With good jobs scarce and with a restive population looking to Congress to initiate some action to alleviate the loss of good-paying manufacturing jobs, Senator Ernest F. Hollings (D) of South Carolina introduced legislation that would enable the seven regional Bell companies to carry out their manufacturing in the United States, but would permit them to import 40 percent of the components.

We are in the grip of a serious permanent recession that started more than a decade ago created by government's callous management of our trade affairs in dismantling our manufacturing sector and resulting in thousands of Americans seeking any kind of employment to survive. The making of equipment here could help our workers find meaningful jobs and maintain the slim world lead we have in communications.

The Bush Administration Acts – Against Americans.

The Bush Administration threatened to veto this bill, objecting to the "domestic content" terms on the grounds that it would spark retaliatory action. For what reason would foreigners retaliate if they made 40 percent of the components? Many U.S. makers would be delighted for an opportunity to make 40 percent of the components in Japanese products. What's wrong in saving jobs for Americans?

The European Community is most careful to ensure the survival of their industry, realizing how great a source of power lies in good-paying jobs for their citizens. And they do this by carefully monitoring all inroads into their markets by foreigners. In the Japanese auto assembly plants in Great Britain, no more than 35 percent of the components may be of foreign manufacture. *In America,* there is no limit set on imported parts for Japanese auto assembly plants. *Imported parts comprise as much as 70 percent of the finished car.*

Young Americans Face A Grim Future

Unlike their fathers, who after leaving high school or college found employment to meet their wishes, our youth are beset with uncertain futures. The factories that paid nice wages with promises of moving up the ranks to higher levels of income are no longer in operation. What employment is available for high school graduates with no specific skills are the low, dead-end service jobs paying wages barely above minimum wage.

When these young people marry, the wives are forced to seek part-time employment to help meet their living needs. The statistics reveal the average work time young families put in is over 3400 hours a year. The average work year for one job is 2000 hours.

Americans in all walks of life seem to share a common need. The scarcity of opportunities to fulfill their hopes for themselves and their families and the grim reality that they may never own that house, send their kids to college, plan that retirement place, and enjoy some of the benefits their parents achieved weighs heavily on their spirits. They look for solace in lotteries and games of chance to lift up their standard of living.

Another fact that our economists are now realizing *is that people with less income spend less. Since 65 percent of our Gross National Product* reflects consumer spending, the end result is a decline in consumption and sales. This reduction in consumer buying habits is not a temporary phase, but one which is related to jobs and net income. With our weakened industrial base, the next decade promises lean times for retailers and business.

Americans love automobiles, and most of all they want to be able to buy new ones frequently, the kind that are loaded with gadgets. As a strong indication of what lies ahead, new car dealers are seeing business in used cars but only a trickle of new car sales. Discounters, stores that deal in used clothing and other articles, are doing a brisk business. Retailers of the better and higher priced goods are going bankrupt in many cases.

Revisiting The Past

I grew up during the Great Depression. I saw at first hand how the excesses of the 1920s spawned the collapse of the economy and the shattering of the financial structure of the nation. And yet, I am an optimist about our future, just as I was in the 1930s.

In this period of the early 1930s, the public learned how to stretch resources. You bought used tires, changed your own oil, washed your own car, ate at home, bought clothing sparingly with the accent on the basics, went to inexpensive plays. The WPA plays produced by Orson Welles charged twenty-five cents a performance! You learned that family and friends were very necessary and rounded out life.

In that era, former executives in Wall Street were selling apples for a living. Jobs were scarce, wages were small, and hopes dim. To survive, many families resorted to taking in "homework" or manufacturing products in the house to earn a few dollars. It took the courage of President Franklin Roosevelt to enact legislation that restored public confidence, provided higher wages for forty hours a week (the average worker had worked six days a week averaging 54 hours), created Unemployment Insurance, the Social Security system, the Federal Deposit Insurance, and a number of measures that saved the capitalistic system in America.

It took years for the nation to rebuild under the "New Deal" as the Roosevelt actions were called. But there was new hope and "Yankee Ingenuity" flourished. Spurred on by people who had visions of building a better life, new products were created that became the landmark of America throughout the world. MADE IN THE U.S.A. was the universal acceptable quality seal and stood for a country that was strong and creative. We were the hope of the world, and American techniques were copied abroad wherever there was industry.

Meaningful Paying Jobs Were Available – If You Wanted To Work During The 1950s-1970s!

Today economists cite the recession as the cause of our current economic decline. They study charts of the past and make forecasts for recovery without factoring in the vast industrial changes that occurred in the 1980s. *Past recoveries were predictable because in place were industries capable of providing work and security for our people.* WE NO LONGER HAVE THE INDUSTRIAL POWER TO MEET THE ECONOMIC NEEDS OF OUR CITIZENS.

HOW DID ALL THIS CHANGE?

A look at history will identify the root cause of our industrial decline.

Following World War II, America, under the Marshall Plan, rebuilt industrial facilities in Western Europe which were shattered by the war. We also gave Japan large amounts of financial aid to rebuild its factories. We were extremely confident of our international role as the greatest industrial machine the world had ever seen and made a number of assumptions that failed to realize our unchallenged domination of world markets would be diluted.

A strong factor in our thinking lay with the staggering production capacity we mustered during World War II. *We built 1000 airplanes a week, launched one ocean-going vessel a day, built 100,000 tanks a year, and manufactured arms, supplies, trucks, clothing, and a multitude of products for all the allies.*

The above reflected the industrial might of America during the 1950s and 1960s. In this heady environment, our government launched the creation of new industries throughout the world through bank loans and urging domestic manufacturers to invest in plants abroad. The conviction was we could compete against all and sundry. What was not factored in our planning was that we were creating competition for world *trade and for the first time competition at home.*

Our government decided that a Free Trade Policy would be good for others and ourselves. Free trade means unrestrained commerce between nations. The theory was that all the parties would operate under the same rules.

The catastrophic reality is that all our trading partners welcomed American naivete and moved into our markets, freely capturing major industry market shares with the blessing of our government. Our trading partners did not oblige us, but effectively closed their markets to our products.

The father of the free-trade concept was an eighteenth century economist, Adam Smith, who conceived the idea that if a nation had industrial facilities it should secure raw materials from a nation with no manufacturing facilities and then sell back to that country the finished product — at a nice profit. It worked out well for years for nations like Great Britain, ruling large colonies dependent on the British for finished goods. Adam Smith's World was entirely different than our world, but strangely enough our country and others are still influenced by his thinking.

In 1958, with trade growing, the free nations of the world joined together to establish the rules under which they would operate. This gave birth to the General Agreements on Trade and Tariffs, or GATT as it is commonly called.

For a period of time, the U.S. did not feel much competition from its trading partners since their industrial base was still in the formative stage. But as the competition eyed our markets, they targeted the products they wanted to make to create jobs for their people.

The apparel industry was an early major target. The Asian countries had countless millions of workers available, easily trained to produce dresses, sweaters, blouses, hats, skirts, shirts, and suits. Pay for workers was as low as six cents an hour.

The impact of this low-cost merchandise, produced under conditions illegal in the U.S., had a severe impact on many industries. To illustrate the huge impact this had on American jobs consider the following:

1978 —	workers in textiles	999,000
	workers in apparel	1,332,000
1990 —	workers in textiles	682,000
	workers in apparel	1,003,000
	Total direct jobs lost	540,000

(Source: U.S. Department of Labor Statistics Published by American Textile Manufacturers Institute, Inc., March, 1991)

South Korea, Hong Kong, and Japan in the early 1970s selected apparel for their "entry" because it was labor intensive. Their costs were but a fraction of ours. American products are made subject to minimum wages and above, health and pension plans, and a host of governmental regulations on hours and working conditions. **The exporting countries paid their labor as little as six cents an hour and often used child labor working under terrible conditions illegal in the U.S.**

This cheap merchandise attracted American retailers and the trend of foreign goods began on a large scale. American manufacturers were suddenly under siege, and they petitioned our government for aid. But U.S. officials were convinced that keeping our market open would be good — it would make our producers more competitive and give the consumer low-priced products. To this theory was added the article of faith that the *market-place should determine the survivor.*

What the administrations past and present did not comprehend, or refused to accept, **was that exporting countries did not operate under the same rules as did domestic producers. U.S. manufacturers simply could not compete unless the American labor force was compelled to work for the same wages as did the Asian countries.**

Obviously, American workers were not ready to work for a few cents a day in order to fulfill an unrealistic government policy.

During the Reagan and now the Bush Administrations, the 1980s saw a tremendous surge of imported products from other countries pouring into our markets — all generally unrestrained. The largest trade deficits in our history were created during this period. We soon owed over 700 billion dollars to others, making us the world's greatest debtor nation. When Carter left office just a few years earlier, we were a creditor nation.

Foreign imports made massive inroads in many of our labor-intensive industries: apparel, shoes, autos, construction equipment, photo-copiers, cameras, household equipment, electronics, airplanes, tractors, cranes, machine tools, glass, ceramics, steel, and countless other products. We experienced a massive assault on our industries by foreign manufacturers from all over the globe. This invasion was bad for our workers, it was bad for our manufacturers, and it was bad for the entire American economy.

Some industries were wiped out. The early targets by these low-cost producers were the apparel and shoe industries. Brazil went after the shoe industry, and her shoe exports reached over $1 billion in one year. Taiwan and China joined in, and now 83 percent of all shoes sold in America are imports.

Today 50 foreign countries are shipping sweaters into our market. They now control 75 percent of the market.

Read The Labels In Products At The Retail Level

When one manufacturing job is lost, industrial engineers have determined that 2.5 other jobs are lost.

The suppliers of raw materials, factory parts, transportation, fuel, building maintenance, insurance, product materials, legal, banking, and accounting services are affected. A vast ripple effect of lost jobs develops after one factory shuts down.

The Children's Defense Fund reports that a new study reveals 20 percent of all children in America now live in poverty, of which the majority are white. The report attributes this problem to low wages.

In this shifting or "exporting" of jobs overseas, no sector of our work force is escaping unscathed. The worker on the production line, the supervisor, the manager, the clerical staff, and the managing director find themselves in the same predicament — seeking employment.

The semiskilled production workers with skills and long years of service confined to a particular industry are hard pressed to find employment providing the wages earned on the lost job.

Because of depressed incomes due to loss of higher paying manufacturing jobs, local community service organizations are reporting increasing requests for food aid from working parents. The number of families with children joining the ranks of the homeless has risen enormously. The service agencies report many of these families cannot afford the high rents for apartments and resort to sleeping in cars.

Where Is "The Better Life" For Our Citizens Promised By Our Political Leaders?

Our government has contended that we should reconcile our role in today's economic world to a service-oriented society. Let the other nations produce cheap goods, and we will be able to buy their products, providing plenty of consumer goods for our citizens.

Let's look at the jobs the service sector offers to

the unskilled: McDonald's, Burger King, Pizza Hut,
gas station attendants, super-markets, shopping malls,
bank clerks, grass-cutters, and window-washers. The
wages paid for these menial jobs are barely above the
minimum prescribed by law. What of the future?

Now many companies are transferring their
record-keeping to far-off places like the Philippines
and Ireland for cheap labor. What future is there in the
service job area for the great masses of the American
public?

A recent TV program interviewed American students who spent six months in Russia to better understand the Russian lifestyle. When questioned about
their impressions, the American students commented
that the Russian people had no hope because the work
they did was unrewarding and led to a dead end. This
is the prescription our government is writing for our
own people.

Yes, there are needs for hi-tech entrepreneurs,
computer operators, lawyers, accountants, bankers,
and brokers, but these needs do not provide employment for most of our people.

Let's examine the jobs given up under the "Free
Market Policy" espoused by our government:

Auto industry, steel, textiles, farming, electronics, building trades, heavy equipment, tractors, cranes,
trucks, machine tools, aircraft, optical equipment,
glass, ceramics, copper, coal, iron, and railroads. The
so-called "blotting paper" industries, which employed
millions of rank-and-file Americans, are all but gone.

Imports Take Over Our Market For
Basic Items And Our Exotic Weaponry

TVs and recorders 100 percent, shoes 83 percent,
apparel 65 percent, oil 55 percent, many electronic
items 100 percent, and numerous household items —
all imported.

And of the nineteen exotic weapons used during the Gulf War, seventeen could not function without parts from foreigners. During World War II, we manufactured 95 percent of all the electronic parts needed for our weaponry.

Our Leaders Do Not Comprehend Manufacturing

A Manufacturing Expert Looks At Industry In America

Rodman C. Wilson, of his management consulting firm with many clients in the Fortune 500, makes some pertinent observations:

"Another example of plant shutdowns was in Louisville, Kentucky, where there is a corporate facility referred to as Appliance Park. In its heyday, it was reported to have 26,000 employees. During my first visit, I found that through closings and transfers of production overseas, they were down to about 13,000. The last I heard about staffing at this facility, their numbers were further reduced to about 9,000. Picture the impact on housing sales and construction, auto sales, furniture, food, and the ability of people to pay taxes to support the police, fire, school, and other services.

"When I consulted for the ball bearing plants of a major U.S. company, I found the Japanese decided to make only small standard bearings using a simple automated line. Since the U.S. company had not upgraded their facilities in years, they could not compete, and so they stopped making those items. The U.S. plants then had to absorb the overhead that the items once covered, which increased their cost and forced them to raise prices. This in turn opened the door for competition to move up to the next sizes, again with the latest equipment.

"When (foreigners) decided to enter the copier

market, they started with a small table model priced at about half the price of those produced by Xerox. We stopped making a unit to compete with this size, allowing them the entry in sales, distribution, and repair facilities. With this start, they began to produce more sophisticated models, and today they can sort, collate, copy both sides, produce in color, etc."

Limited Market For The
Highly-Skilled Workers

The work force required for the hi-tech industries is estimated to total 20 percent of available labor. *What provision is made for the 80 percent remaining who are not needed or do not qualify for these highly skilled jobs?*

During my term in office as President of The National Knitwear and Sportwear Association, I was part of a lobbying effort in Washington, D.C.

I recall one meeting with the chief legislative aide to a New Jersey Senator. He commented that at a meeting of a "think tank" group the idea was put forth that *all labor intensive industry in America was expendable.* I was aghast.

"What will you do with the 2.5 million skilled and semiskilled workers in the textile-apparel industry who would lose their jobs?" I asked.

The response was "they will find other work!"

No Other Country In The World
Has Sacrificed Its Manufacturing Strength
As Has The U.S. Government

As a manufacturer of knitwear for over fifty years, I lived through the various stages of government trade policy and can testify that we saw our market given to foreigners with little help from the government.

The chief exporter of jobs is our government.

The jobs that were available in abundance in past decades for our youth, our blue-collar factory workers, our semiskilled minorities, the newly arrived immigrants, our managers, our executives, and our white-collar workers are no longer available. The highly touted service sector is simply no substitute for a nation of producers of goods.

As we enter the '90s, the economic future for most Americans is bleak because our leaders have been deluded by unworkable theories.

Perhaps the answer rests with:

David Halberstam in his book *The Next Century* (William Morrow and Company, pages 67-68) states:

> "We did not realize that America had become an empire, run by men suited to running empires, men who did not necessarily value the truth. They were far too grand for that; they valued power over truth. They had created their own truth: In power there was truth."

Will they listen to truth, and will they change?

WHERE HAVE ALL THE JOBS GONE IN AMERICA?

What Is Manufacturing?

Jobs are now the paramount concern for most Americans, blue-collar workers, and executives alike. The decline of our industrial base has created vast unemployment for managers on a scale only experienced during the Great Depression. Unemployed people do not spend, and since public spending accounts for 65 percent of our Gross National Product, recoveries from recessions are slow indeed.

Since ancient times, the human race has been engaged in producing objects to serve its needs. A trip to the museums reveals the creations developed by our ancestors. Peoples who created objects were sought out for trade, and the ancients traveled perilous seas to buy these products.

In our times, the basis of a healthy economy deals with the scope and nature of "things" we make. Manufacturing requires capital, manpower, space, raw materials, and a host of services. It is the parent of new industries spawned from the growing hunger of new products.

In the manufacturing process, skills required vary dependent on the industry and products made. At the bottom of the ladder, workers are needed with minor skills, and progressively more skills and education are required. Today economic theorists stress that we need to accent a higher level of education and to accept a role of providing hi-tech specialists to add to the value of the product if we are to survive in the fierce industrial international competition.

We need to move in that direction, but the role suggested assumes that the entire work force would have to meet that criterion. Not every industry requires highly trained specialists in all the operations performed. Nor can we assume that all workers can become highly trained specialists. We need a large work force to meet the "nuts and bolts" part of our economy.

A new study arrived at the conclusion that one out of seven Americans is functionally illiterate. Assuming this conclusion is correct, the problem for our society is to factor in all our planning that jobs must be available in depth to give the uneducated and the unskilled an opportunity to earn a living. Other countries are realistically seeking to industrialize in areas that will provide employment for their masses. Countries like China, India, the Philippines, South Korea, Thailand, and Malaysia turn to producing products requiring much labor to give their people work.

As an example, in America, the textile apparel industry is labor intensive in many sectors and could utilize the skills now available. In our economic planning, it is vital to factor in the needs and skills of our existing work force. The economic theorists who charge we are failing to meet the challenge posed by foreigners have no experience in the real world of manufacturing.

Unrestrained Immigration –
What Jobs Available?

We are the most liberal country in the world, permitting people from all countries to enter our shores. Many of the newcomers do not speak our language, have limited skills, and quickly become wards of the state unless work is available. In the past, prior to our free trade policy which has resulted in the exportation of our manufacturing base on a massive scale, these new prospective citizens found jobs in our factories and were able to exist free of welfare.

In my industry, immigrants from Germany and Italy were the chief source of labor during the 1930s to the 1960s. As they achieved economic security and were able to educate their children, we lost this class of labor. The Hispanics from Puerto Rico and Cuba then became our chief source of labor. They learned on the job, and many prospered. The jobs were there.

But government trade policies created a flood of cheap labor products from China, South Korea, Taiwan, Hong Kong, and India that created unfair competition for our industry and a host of others. About 75 percent of the knitwear producers were forced out of business. The result of lost industries has created staggering increases in the welfare roles and financial hardships for many of our cities.

In the past decades prior to the 1970s, our youth with limited schooling could find employment in our factories. The opportunity to acquire skills on the job were plentiful, and many an industry leader emerged from the ranks. Plants producing shoes, apparel, steel, autos, TVs, cameras, electronic, and household products were a source of work. *The workers had hope. It was possible to move up in the ranks and acquire the good things their parents achieved.*

*Manufacturing Is The Foundation
Of An Industrial Nation*

From this sector are created new products requiring all forms of labor with varying degrees of skills. New emerging industries *add to the economic muscle, making a nation strong.* Every free nation recognizes this basic truth and moves to industrialize. This is the history of America. To abdicate this truth is to relegate our country to a minor economic status dependent on foreigners for our basic needs.

Why Does Every Developing Country Industrialize?

Manufacturing creates jobs and increases wealth, raising the standard of living of its citizens. Vast numbers of workers in China, India, Sri Lanka, Philippines, Indonesia, and other Asian countries are now being employed for pennies a day to manufacture products for shipment to America, Europe, and elsewhere.

The need to find markets for their products creates competition for industrialized countries where the cost of producing is far greater. The less-developed countries do not have to deal with high wages (China pays ten cents an hour, Sri Lanka six cents). Nor are they burdened with a host of government and environmental regulations.

The established nations with greater affluence have the buying power and become the target for the low-cost foreign producers. How does one control these forces now converging everywhere on the world markets?

The free-world nations set up a mechanism called The General Agreement on Tariffs and Trade designed to *create an orderly flow of trade between nations. It is important to note the word orderly.*

How does the United States deal with the problem? A Trade Representative is appointed by the President to negotiate trade agreements. These agreements result from complaints registered by American manufacturers faced with inroads of their market by low-cost foreign goods.

Represented in the trade negotiations are the State, Commerce, and Treasury Departments. Industries affected are consulted but do not participate in the direct negotiations. The chief architect of trade policy is the State Department. During my involvement in the trade process, the quota positions recommended by our manufacturers were never accepted by the U.S. negotiators.

A Government Fantasy – Free Trade

Free trade in theory means unrestrained commerce between nations. If Japan wants to ship four million autos into our market or Brazil wants to ship ten million pairs of shoes or China sends 100,000,000 pieces of apparel, they are free to do so with few restraints. Quotas are in force for some products, but the quantities given are so enormous the U.S. market is dominated by these shipments.

The theory behind this policy is that *we will see an increase in American jobs because the foreigners will buy our products with the dollars they accumulate.* Another theory our government has is that all other nations we trade with will also follow the same pattern and open their markets to us. The record is quite clear: *Our trading partners don't practice free trade, and we have the trade deficits to prove it.* So the results are hidden in a smoke screen of denial, and people don't know where the jobs have gone.

The many sectors of our country experiencing loss of basic and hi-tech industries to foreigners disprove these government theories that Free Trade has benefited Americans.

Recent editorials in leading newspapers make a plea for free trade on the grounds that we will create jobs in depressed countries. According to our government's reports, we absorb 64 percent of all exports from the less-developed countries. The European Community absorbs 25 percent and Japan three percent. How much more are we to take from our citizens? Should not all nations assume a greater share in helping the depressed countries?

A Recent News Headline: Bridgeport, Connecticut, Applies For Relief Under Bankruptcy Procedures. Mayor Citing Lost Industries Created Sharp Decline In Revenues. This Is A First Case Of A Community Taking Such Action.

Free trade is a fantasy. It is astounding to hear legislators publicly stating "I believe in free trade" after it has created such economic turmoil in the U.S. Foreigners have poured in low-cost products and forced our plants to close to the extent that our leaders have turned to the tariff agreement (GATT) to enforce rules to equalize the trade relationship.

In 1990, 48 additional textile plants closed with a loss of 34,000 jobs with employment falling to 681,000 jobs — the lowest since statistics began in 1939. (Source: American Textile Manufacturers Institute, Inc., March, 1991.)

One wonders which branch of our government reads these statistics and do they relate to them?

The problem is that we maintain the "open market policy" but OUR TRADING PARTNERS DO NOT.

The trade deficit with the balance of trade favoring our trading partners tells the story —

We imported this much
more than we sold in a
single year:

COUNTRY	DEFICIT AS OF 12/31/91
Germany	$ 4.900 BILLION
Italy	3.200 "
Japan	43.413 "
Thailand	2.367 "
Hong Kong	1.506 "
Taiwan	9.854 "
South Korea	1.506 "
China	12.369 "

(Source: United States Department of Commerce)

Our failure to demand a "Fair Trade" relationship from our partners has created the trade imbalance. Unfortunately for us, our bureaucrats are not
fired for poor performance as is the case in the business world.

We now owe others $700 billion and are the
world's largest debtor nation. In 1980, we were a
creditor nation.

One wonders with amazement how a govern-
ment, like the United States, can sacrifice the livelihood of its citizens by adhering to a free trade policy
that has eroded the foundations of a once-mighty
American Industrial machine which was the source
of security for countless American families.

A domestic manufacturer will not invest in new
plants when exposed to imports, particularly when he
knows our government will disregard his declining
domestic market position. The callousness of the
government's position "let the marketplace determine
the survivor" has generated a "hollowing of American
industry," reflecting a decline in our manufacturing

base in an endless number of products. The Japanese marvel at the naivete of our government in ignoring the basic tenets governing survival in the tough economic trading climate that exists today.

Expand Your American Plant – Why?

Manufacturers make their domestic expansion plans only if market conditions exist to insure confidence that their investments are not subject to theoretical political policies that could destroy their market position. Why build a plant when tomorrow our government will conclude a trade agreement with a foreign low-labor producer that will wipe out your market share?

I was a knitwear manufacturer for 50 years. Our plans to enlarge production came to a halt when we experienced the low-cost competition from companies like South Korea, Hong Hong, Taiwan, China, and others. I laid off American workers so that foreign workers could have their jobs.

My customers found they could buy sweaters from foreigners for 60 percent less than mine. I could not hire the same cheap labor as my foreign competitors, who were favored by our government. Had I paid their kind of wages and maintained my plants according to their safety standards, I would probably have been sent to prison. We and our entire industry lost market share. Today the sweater industry is 25 percent the size it was in the 1970s. This chain of events has been repeated in every American industry, and that is why there are no decent jobs left for our citizens.

When American industries submitted the damaging import data to the U.S. Trade Representative requesting realistic quotas to preserve industry and jobs, all pleas fell on deaf ears. We were unable to change a policy dedicated to giving foreigners primary access to our market.

Small business is the backbone of America. There are 18 million small companies in America that create two out of three new jobs, create most of the new technology, pay more taxes, contribute 40 percent of our production, and most new products. Does Washington, D.C. know?

Imports Now Control 16 Percent Of
Our Gross National Product

IMPORTS OF TEXTILES AND APPAREL ROSE 19 PERCENT DURING THE CARTER TENURE AND 96 PERCENT DURING REAGAN'S FIRST TERM IN OFFICE. REAGAN AS PRESIDENTIAL CANDIDATE PROMISED TO "SAVE AMERICAN JOBS." THE SAME TREND CONTINUES IN THE BUSH ADMINISTRATION.

Learn To Be More Competitive
Says Our Government

Over the years, the standard of living in America had risen steadily. Legislation established numerous controls over the manufacturing process; basic social benefits covering health care and pensions are in place — all costly but necessary for the welfare of our citizens.

Foreigners in the Far East have few or no regulations governing manufacturing — in fact, they subsidize their industries to ensure their survival. If U.S. industry is to be competitive, wages would have to be reduced and all benefits eliminated. In essence, we would have to operate like China, reducing the entire standard of living for all our workers. In Shekou, China, it is reported children as young as ten are working in toy factories up to 14 and 15 hours a day at salaries of $10 a month.

Do the Washington bureaucrat policy-makers comprehend this? And do they even care? Since they have no experience in the real world, they fall back on empty slogans established by our Administration, "free trade will benefit everyone."

OVER 50 FOREIGN COUNTRIES SHIP KNIT PRODUCTS INTO AMERICA

U.S. Multinational Manufacturers Love Free Trade

Following World War II, the multinational manufacturers in America saw an opportunity to set up plants in Japan and in Europe to capitalize on cheap labor and operating costs. The State Department urged this move, and the exodus to manufacture abroad was accelerated. The Free Trade policy made it more attractive since the products manufactured could be returned for sale in America with few or no restraints, generating huge profits for retailers.

"Fortune 500" Companies Desert America

The "Fortune 500" companies are now investing more abroad than in the U.S. It is reported in 1990 they set up 271 new projects. This was up 25 percent from 1989 and increased their foreign investments in new plants to $54.9 billion from $48.9 billion in 1989. (Source: U.S. Department of Commerce, Bureau of Economic Analysis.) The reason for this overseas growth is not well understood here by average citizens.

Smaller U.S. companies are getting into the act. They acquired both in Britain and on the continent 185 companies valued at $15.2 billion, almost double the 1988 level. (Source: Translink's European Deal Review).

The extent of this migration is portrayed daily in the news media with data covering U.S. plant closings and the shifting of manufacturing operations overseas.

- General Electric is reported to have large manufacturing operations in Singapore.
- Ford Motor has a large plant in Mexico.
- IBM moved its $10 billion communications division to Europe.
- The U.S. auto-makers import more than they export.
- Boeing imported three percent of its parts in 1980. In 1987, it imported 28 percent.
- U.S. data-input firms export work to use cheap Philippine Islands labor. College grads are paid $150 a month.

The desire for greater profits has driven U.S. corporations to manufacture abroad. Corporate America practices no allegiance to the welfare of Americans. The Free Trade Policy makes it easy to ship back into the U.S. products made abroad. The downgrading by our government of manufacturing and the false notion we can survive as a service-oriented society has reduced the United States to its current dependence on foreigners for money to balance our federal deficits and to supply us with our basic needs.

In his book *The Next Century* (William Morrow and Company, Inc.), David Halberstam quotes Kazuo Inamuri, President of Kyota Ceramics, world re-known manufacturer with five factories in America alone: *"College grads are too theoretical. They think factories are distant and unimportant. They need to learn the importance of making something and of producing something. Only then are they valuable."*

The Kyota Ceramics are unequaled in quality and service. Mr. Inamuri has dignified the ancient art of creating products useful to our civilization. He also feels, however, it is easy to fall from grace. Our auto industry is a vivid example of this truth.

We now import 83 percent of the shoes sold in this country. Are imported shoes less expensive? Our government says so. What price labels do they read? Our parents will tell how they could purchase shoes from Thom McCan for $4.75 a pair. I remember purchasing fine shoes during the 1970s from Whitehouse & Hardy for $25.00 a pair. Recently when I purchased a pair of galoshes, the price was $20.00, up from $5.00 a pair. What happened?

When market domination passes into foreign hands, foreigners can control prices. This has happened in the shoe industry and in other industries. Today there are no cheap shoes. Prices range from $80.00 to hundreds of dollars per pair. How can workers earning minimum wages afford these prices?

How does our government respond to the obvious fact that there are no cheap shoe imports to save the American consumer money? Regarding sweaters, I can testify that as late as 1978, you could purchase quality sweaters from $10.00 to $25.00 in good retail establishments. The exporting countries, with their partner, the American retailers, teamed up to increase the markups on sweaters from a domestic rate of 100 percent to as high as 700 percent and higher on imported sweaters.

Here Is How The American Consumer Gets Cheated

If a retailer purchased a sweater from a domestic producer for $5.00, he sold it for $10.00. Purchasing the same or similar sweater from China for $2.75, he would sell it for $10.00, using a higher markup. But now markups are even higher.

One of the myths our government proclaims is that control of imports will cost the consumer billions of dollars annually. The markup data has been researched by Congressional Committees, industry, and unions and all adds up to the same truths — there is no saving for the American consumer.

With the decline in domestic shoe manufacturers, the prices moved up dramatically at the retail level. The medical profession, the podiatrists, are doing a booming business. Imported shoes sizes vary from country to country, creating many foot problems.

In 1990, 47 shoe manufacturing plants in America closed down. (Source: U.S. Department of Commerce.)

When Congress began to feel pressure from the public and saw the growing size of the trade deficit, it finally acted and passed the Omnibus Trade Bill in 1987. Supposedly, this bill would correct trade inequities and save American jobs, but the bill had so many loopholes that it failed.

For years our Trade Representatives had "jawboned" Japanese officials to open up its markets. Japanese leaders promised "to study the situation," but after years of discussions little progress was made. Japan bought our lumber, *not the finished product, some beef, fish, and scrap metal.* But when we asked to participate in the major airport construction in Japan, we were told "Japan's soil is holy. We do not permit foreigners to handle it."

Section 301 of the Omnibus Trade Bill provided the mechanism for the President to impose sanctions on trading partners who practice unfair trade with the U.S. For years our rice growers had attempted to sell rice to Japan with no success. The Japanese public was paying five times the price of rice sold in America. When the appeal was made to the President to act, he resorted to the flaw in the Bill which permitted him *not to retaliate if it affected national interest.* The appeal of our rice growers was denied.

If Free Trade Helps Everyone, Why Can't We Sell Rice To Japan?

In 1990, our rice growers displayed a few pounds of American rice samples at an exhibit in Japan. The Japanese authorities *threatened to jail the American exhibitors if the samples were not removed. Our people were forced to do so and our government did nothing.*

Not a day passes in our country without displays, advertisements, TV commercials — you name it — extolling the virtues of Japanese products. Do we restrain the Japanese?

Note the difference:

Japan wanted to protect their rice farmers and acted to do so.

The American government demonstrated a lack of will to make the choices we expect of elected officials.

Japan is now openly exhibiting contempt for America in public statements, and you can now read an English translation of the new book published in Japan, *The Japan That Can Say No: Why Japan Will Be First Among Equals* by Ishihara, Shintaro (Simon & Schuster, New York, 1991).

The China Deal

China "opened to America" by some of the overtures made by former President Nixon and President George Bush some years ago. Contact with the West induced China to develop an export program of manufactured goods to earn hard currency. Apparel is labor intensive, and China proceeded to solicit business on sweaters and other items.

In the mid-1970s, China began submitting its first sweater samples to U.S. retailers. I inspected some of the first sweaters submitted and noted the lack of fashion and fit in their garments. The Chinese women have different physical proportions than our women, and the sweaters were rather primitive and unappealing. But our retailers, the buyers of low-cost import products, were enchanted by the cheap prices and gave the Chinese detailed specifications to follow. In fact, designers were sent to the Far East to educate the producers regarding American taste.

The Chinese learned quickly and subsequent samples conformed to American specifications. So close did they follow the details that flaws in the domestic fabric were duplicated.

China's shipments to the U.S. in the later 1970s began to grow at an alarming rate. They had no quotas and *could ship as many as they could sell, knowing that all quota negotiations would be based on the existing shipments.* Our industry made representation to our Trade Representative and to President Carter, but after several years quotas were established. However, China had gotten its foot "in the door," and from then on it was their game and they played hard ball.

Evasion Of Trade Quotas Destroys Jobs

Apparel became a major target for foreign exporters. The mounting pressure of these cheap-labor products created such pressure on American makers that our government was forced to seek other means to prevent collapse of the textile apparel industry, the largest employer in America. Sweaters made of acrylic were popular in America and sweaters of cotton increasingly so, but China and other exporters decided they wanted a bigger share of our market than established quotas would permit, so they developed a scheme to circumvent quotas.

The nettle plant or ramie is grown in abundance in the Far East. It could be blended with acrylic and other fibers, and in a sweater can be made to look and feel somewhat like an all-cotton version. The ramie blend, however, does not quite have the quality look of a 100-percent cotton fabric, *but it is cheaper and there was no quota on this blend.*

Under The General Agreement on Tariffs and Trade, the Multi-Fibre Agreement (MFA) was established to address itself to the task of developing orderly bilateral trade agreements for textile apparel products. The Multi-Fibre Agreement established quotas on products that were disrupting our markets. The quotas, however, were quite generous and gave the exporter a good piece of our market.

In the case of sweaters, the quota listing was for sweaters of cotton or acrylic fibers. The Far East, led by China, began shipping ramie-blend sweaters into our market in enormous quantities. The ramie-blend sweaters shipped into our market in 1982 totaled 6.3 million. In 1986, it ballooned to 132.4 million, all shipped outside the quota allotment!

How could this happen? Our government said that since the system applied to *cotton sweaters only, and not to sweaters which were in chief value of ramie, no action could be taken.* For several years, our government refused to reconsider its position. The retailer and the consumer purchased this garment as if it were cotton. Because our government took several years to act, the total number of ramie-cotton sweaters *exceeded the entire domestic U.S. sweater production in that year.*

Is this the end? No — after much controversy — and delayed international negotiations, quotas were established on the ramie-blend — again after the damage was done. *Quotas were never "rolled back or reduced."* China's quota on one category of sweaters was 12 million for 1987. They overshipped this quota by 12 million, and U.S. Customs caught this and placed the overshipment in embargo. We inquired what disposition would be made of the overshipment, and our government assured everyone — including Congress, which was getting into the act — the additional sweaters would be placed against the new agreement being negotiated with China.

Was it done? Well, our government solved this "overshipment" problem by retroactively increasing the quota — presto — no overshipment. This increased the 1987 quota for China on this one category to 24 million.

This decision *on this one item (China had more categories)* gave China 15 percent of the total domestic sweater market, forcing more knitting mills out of business.

In response to this government action, Senator Ernest F. Hollings was quoted in the December 19, 1987, *Congressional Record - Senate* as follows:

". . . the current bilateral textile and apparel agreement with the People's Republic of China expires at the end of this month . . . yet despite the contrived appearance of drawn-out negotiations, I have ample reason to believe — based on extensive conversations with textile executives — that the end-product has long since been agreed to and that it is a sweetheart deal for the Chinese.

"Mr. President, the American people have a right to expect good-faith, tough-minded bargaining from our negotiators and from the Office of the Special Trade Representative. Regrettably, however, it is clear *that their alleged bargaining with the Chinese has been nothing more than a charade. The negotiation process has been conducted so as to create the perception of hard bargaining, but in reality these negotiations have been a sham.*

"*Mr. President, the fault does not lie entirely with the negotiators themselves. They are simply following instructions handed down from on high within the administration. The fix is in, and I fear that we are being set up for yet another outrageous give-away at great cost to our domestic textile and apparel industry."*

To continue, Senator Hollings comments:

". . . our negotiators . . . are working from pre-determined figures for import quotas for textile and apparel categories . . . the administration has sought to satisfy . . . China's clamoring for still larger markets . . . imports . . . are to be substantially increased in many categories."

Continuing,

". . . I would note. . . . Apparently in the beginning of 1987, there was no United States position . . . with the People's Republic of China. Apparently this was changed when Secretary of State George Schulz visited China last April. But developments in the bilateral discussions since that visit indicate a clear pattern of preemptive concessions by the American negotiators."

These comments confirm the conviction of the many industries in America that "deals are made" by the State Department resulting in exporting jobs and continuing the emasculation of our manufacturing position. It is noteworthy to hear Senator Hollings reaction to the lack of logic in the judgment used by our negotiators:

"The rationale for giving the People's Republic of China . . . even larger aggregate totals was that we had given larger aggregate totals to two other countries. In other words, the justification for the China sell-out was, that, well, we had already given huge quotas to other countries so we had to give China more . . . is it any wonder this nation is losing its shirt to foreign competition?"

Senator Hollings is Chairman of the Senate Committee on Commerce and Transportation.

The administration's decision to continue "Most Favored Nation" treatment for China created a storm in Congress. Particular stress was made of the *"gulag labor"* employed by China and its total disregard of our proprietary rights, its selling missiles to Syria and

Pakistan, and the suppression of its people.

If China was to be removed from this favored position, it is estimated that a "T-shirt" duty would raise from 21 percent to 91 percent. So? The retailer would employ less than his high markup, and the end result to the American consumer would be unchanged. As Senator Patrick Monyihan of New York said in a recent interview regarding the China problem, we should observe the standards of the world community in making policy decisions.

China's balance of trade is expected to reach $15 billion in 1991 — second to Japan. China is using the dollars earned to buy from others — not the U.S.

Why You Can't Always Believe Some Government Statistics

Dr. Janet L. Norwood, Commissioner of Labor Statistics, has been quite candid on the question of government statistics: "We know the unemployment rate by itself does not always reflect adequately the problems experienced by some groups of our population."

If you are no longer eligible for unemployment benefits, you are not counted as unemployed. Or if you are an early retiree, or part of the growing number of youths not working, you are not considered unemployed.

On the other hand, if you work one hour a month, you are considered employed!

During the 1970s, three percent unemployment was considered intolerable.

Recent articles deal with the misleading government statistics. Budget cuts and neglect have left the main producers of government statistics, the Labor and Commerce Departments, unable to track a rapidly shifting economy. The economy was actually declining at a troubling 3.1 percent pace in the fourth quarter of 1989, nearly twice as fast as initially estimated.

The problem with the government's numbers go far beyond a single set of Gross National Product figures. From retail sales to the trade gap, the statistics needed by policy-makers and business are either misleading, late, or just not available. The paucity of accurate and timely information has even more serious consequences for policy debates over such issues as international trade, competitiveness, and health care.

U.S. DEPARTMENT OF COMMERCE OFFICIALS STATE OPENLY THAT CONGRESS IN REDUCING AVAILABLE FUNDS HAS MANDATED CURTAILMENT OF ISSUANCE OF VITAL STATISTICAL DATA.

All this raises a serious question regarding the value of decisions made by Congress and the Administration, if the statistics are flawed. David Stockman, Director of the Office of Management and Budget in President Reagan's first term, describes the difficulties in the budget forming process. His book is entitled *The Triumph of Politics* (Harper and Row).

The Defense Department's decision to continue to make armaments that do not work because they don't want to stop production illustrates the level of thinking of the people we have running the affairs of our nation. We deserve better.

Solution To Free Trade –
Yes. The Government

The U.S. steel industry has long suffered from overcapacity and cut-throat competition from the European Community and the Far East. The EEC had subsidized their steel industry to the extent of $35 billion during the past decade and were constantly dumping surplus production into our market.

Faced with declining domestic steel production needed for armaments, the U.S. Defense Department became alarmed, and at their urging, President Reagan limited foreign producers to 20 percent of the U.S. market. This policy enabled the domestic producers to restructure their operations to become more efficient.

The Reagan decision to introduce "market sharing," that is to say, allocating a portion of our market to domestic producers, shocked the U.S. free-traders who blindly pursued the same old policies advocated by Adam Smith. The assumptions made by this sector of government was that the rest of the world would follow suit and open their markets to our products.

The free-traders brushed aside the truths: The U.S. steel industry, faced with staggering losses, idled plants and annual production reduced from 137 million tons annually and operating at a reduced rate of 77 million tons annually, was on the verge of collapse.

The Market Sharing Concept Worked Despite Dire Predictions Of Retaliation Forecast By The Free-Traders

MANAGED TRADE, AS WAS INITIATED FOR THE STEEL INDUSTRY, IS THE SOLUTION TO HALTING THE DECLINE IN OUR INDUSTRIAL BASE. IT WORKED FOR STEEL, OUR TRADING PARTNERS ACCEPTED IT (THEY PRACTICED MANAGED TRADE – IT WAS THEIR GAME), USING THIS CONCEPT AS A ROLE MODEL WILL REVIVE AMERICA'S ECONOMY.

The Dismal '80s

The Reagan years saw a major swing away from some of the old values. The "fast lane" with the overpowering greed to make "the quick buck" took over. Corporations were obsessed with short-term profits, keeping an eye on the reaction in the financial world to their operations rather than developing long-range plans for product development.

Taxes were reduced, deregulation was in vogue, and leveraged buyouts the new game. Junk bonds were promoted, huge debt incurred, uncontrolled spending increased, rising costs escalated for new homes, yachts, luxury items.

"Money used to talk, now it shrieks," writes Kevin Phillips in his book, *The Politics Of The Rich And Poor* (Random House).

He writes, ". . . at America's universities surveys showed the students were dominated by a single ambition — doing something that could make money. Special causes had failed."

Some additional quotes:

"An imbalance of wealth is now concentrated among the super-rich — one percent of our population."

"Forces lose touch with the public and excessively empower their own elites."

"Upper-tier Americans significantly expanded their share of national wealth while low-income citizens lost ground and Reagan policies were critical to this shift."

Of President Bush: "Bush cannot identify national problems because to do so would identify many of his own party's feelings."

Kevin Phillips was a well-respected political consultant to Republican presidents for years. His comments created a storm in political circles.

The climate he described spawned the gross mismanagement of public funds by the Savings & Loan Thrifts and the banking industry. We do not know the full cost of these excesses which our taxpayers must carry.

Manufacturing did not fare well in a climate of greed and promotion of selfish interests. Many corporate leaders were reluctant to assume the task of nurturing and developing the manufacturing sectors of their companies. It was more glamorous to pursue profits through acquisitions, sale of assets, and stock manipulations. It was easier to "let the Japanese or some foreigner make the products."

The decline in old ethical standards became apparent when former members of the administration and Congress used their past associations to lobby for foreign governments after leaving public office. Many lobbied for their future clients while still in office. This "sleaze" in conduct advertised everything was for sale for a price. It was lamentable to see former President Reagan go to Japan after leaving office to "promote good will" for the sum of $2 million.

Foreigners Gobble Up Our Assets

Flush with dollars received from their favorable trade balances, Japan and European Economic Community members eyed American industry, land, financial institutions, and real estate. Downtown Los Angeles became 50 percent Japanese-owned. The entire Hawaiian waterfront was bought by the Japanese. An estimated 30 percent of U.S. banks are now owned by Japanese. Vast tracts of land with valuable timber is foreign-owned. Large real estate investments such as the Rockefeller Center are now in Japanese hands. Numerous established American manufacturing firms were sold — all for profit.

As American hi-tech plants were being purchased, their new technology enabled the Japanese to "leapfrog" into new areas, saving them vast research sums. Our Defense Department became alarmed and only then did the administration stir to examine some of the purchases. But again, the State Department was involved — on the side of the foreigners. The American public is greatly concerned at choice assets now controlled by foreigners — not so our government.

U.S. Governors And Mayors Go To Japan To Plead For Economic Aid

Faced with plant closings, high unemployment, increased welfare roles, and declining revenues, our municipal and state officials are growing desperate. Knowing little cooperation was to be expected from the Washington bureaucrats, they decided to plead with the Japanese to open manufacturing plants in their cities. All kinds of inducements were offered: free facilities, tax credits, and aid packages.

It is tragic — we beat the Japanese militarily and now we plead for their help to survive economically. Our Washington leaders created the problems for our governors and mayors. They have insulated and isolated themselves from the real needs of Americans. David Halberstam was right. *People running our country valued power over truth. They had created their own truth.*

Want A Job – Move Out Of The Country

The No. 1 job exporter is the U.S. Government. In the midst of a shrinking job market, with plant closings, financial institutions reducing personnel, and the service industries not only cutting back but exporting jobs to cheap labor countries like the Philippines and Jamaica, a government agency, The Overseas Private Investment Corporation, is working hard to get U.S. manufacturers to set up plants abroad.

An article in the press alerted me to the existence of this agency, and a call to Washington, D.C. confirmed its activities. At my request, all the material covering its role was sent at once. This government agency is designed to encourage American business to set up plants abroad, particularly in the "less-developed, friendly countries and areas." To encourage this shifting of investments abroad, the following program is offered by The Overseas Private Investment Corporation:

1) Direct loans ranging from $500,000 to $6 million to small U.S. businesses. These should be companies defined as industrial companies with annual sales of less than $142 million.

2) Loan guaranties available *to all businesses regardless of size could range from $2 to $50 million — all loans backed by the full faith and credit of the United States of America.*

3) The Overseas Private Investment Corporation will insure the investor's risk for

INCONVERTIBILITY:

This protects the investor against the inability to convert into U.S. dollars the local currency received as profits, earnings, or return of capital on an investment.

EXPROPRIATION:

This covers an investor against confiscation or nationalization without compensation.

POLITICAL VIOLENCE:

This covers an investor against losses due to war, revolution, insurrection and civil strife. An investor may elect to cover loss of business income or loss of tangible assets.

The investors buy this insurance coverage from The Overseas Private Investment Corporation (OPIC).

As reported in *The New York Times* (February 18, 1991), Congress has now broadened the role of OPIC to make equity investments for the first time.

Fred E. Zeder, President, is taking a score of top executives, from companies like AT&T, GTE, and Unocal Geothermal, to Panama to explore investment opportunities to "jump start the economy."

It is reported that this agency supported 115 new projects in 35 third world countries last year.

The shifting of manufacturing overseas has reduced the availability of higher paying jobs, not only for the blue-collar worker, but for many highly skilled managers who are unemployed and face a bleak employment future.

In my industry, the knitwear sector of the apparel industry, we saw 75 percent of our market share shifted to countries like Sri Lanka, China, Thailand, and a host of others *with no assistance offered for survival, such as offered by OPIC.*

If the shoe, apparel, electronics, machine tools, and a host of other industries were offered programs created to help them survive in these stressful economic times, our citizens could have hope for the future.

Public opinion polls time and again indicate that the Bush Administration is failing to address the needs of Americans. We respond quickly to the plight of the Kurds at the conclusion of the Gulf War — and that is proper. But many of our citizens are scrounging to eke out a livelihood in an economic climate that offers little hope to rise out of poverty.

Professor Paul Kennedy, of Yale University, writes in his book *The Rise And Fall Of The Great Powers* (Random House):

"Without a rough balance between the competing demands of defense, consumption, and investment, a Great Power is unlikely to preserve its status for long."

America is totally unprepared for the role it has seized as the only super-power.

Unless we can change the thinking and the management of our economic affairs, we must fear for the future of our great country.

We Need An Industrial Policy.

3

THE UNITED STATES STATE DEPARTMENT BUYS ALLIES BY GIVING THEM OUR INDUSTRIES AND JOBS

State Department Pork Barrel Fattens Foreigners

When a Congressman rewards his friends and supporters back home with juicy government contracts or special federal funds, we call it "pork barrel" politics. This type of action is rightfully condemned as shameful and sometimes results in the ouster or jailing of the corrupt Congressman when laws are broken. Political favoritism is vigorously opposed by public interest groups, ethics panels, and others concerned with the welfare of the American nation.

A similar, though unrecognized, problem exists in the State Department. Here, career diplomats practice pork barrel politics on a massive scale with foreign nations. They promise billions of dollars worth of export permits in order to win friends for the United States. In effect, what they give away are U.S. jobs by the millions and U.S. factories by the thousands. This is one major cause of the present decline in the U.S.

economy, although the causes are complex. Our diplomats have given away our jobs in return for military
bases, military alliances, and pledges of international
good will.

A local Congressman hopes to win jobs for his
district by proposing legislation to fund programs for
his constituents. If he can keep a military base open, or
direct a large government contract to factories in his
territory, he may win votes. A career diplomat, on the
other hand, has no constituency. He is a lifetime civil
servant with no election to face and no worries about
job security. Presidents may change, but he remains.

A diplomat who persuades a formerly hostile
nation to sign a peace treaty with the U.S. will win high
accolades and promotion. If the method he uses to
succeed is to promise the foreign government that it
will be allowed to export a million automobiles into
the U.S. or a million tons of steel, this strategy will not
lower his salary or diminish his lifestyle. He does not
care a whit if he puts 10,000 U.S. workers on the
unemployment line. The measure of his success as a
diplomat is the foreign treaty he concludes or the
military alliance he arranges.

Military alliances are important to our welfare as
a nation. Peace treaties and international goodwill are
much needed. But the foreign service should not have
the right to buy goodwill with our factories and our
jobs. Since we regularly conclude hundreds of foreign
agreements with the nations of the world, the State
Department has almost endless opportunities to bar-
gain away our industrial strength in return for diplomatic successes. This long-continued practice has done
much to destroy the American middle class and tar-
nish the American dream. So much has been given
away and bargained away by this time that the economic recession is rapidly accelerating.

During the decade that the industrial heartland
collapsed due to our diplomatic giveaways of agricul-

ture, steel, automobiles, and heavy equipment, the opinion-makers of the East showed little concern. The American heartland became known as the rustbelt, and millions of once-prosperous citizens in middle America descended into genteel poverty. Houses went unpainted; barns decayed; the world's greatest steel works rusted; the factories were silent. Permanent part-time jobs became the norm in middle America, and today husbands and wives struggle with two or three part-time jobs each, while children work when they can.

Permanent Recession Moves to the East Coast

Now the effects of State Department abuse of the economy are beginning to be felt in the East with massive layoffs and permanent job insecurity. Economists puzzle over consumers' lack of courage to buy new cars, houses, and goods of all types. The public is in shock from the rapid decline in living standards. What the Middle West has suffered for many years is now creeping into all parts of the nation.

The East Coast held a virtual monopoly on banking, brokerage, insurance, publishing, corporate headquarters, venture capital, and service industries of all kinds. Service industries were supposed to be immune to the ills of manufacturing. But as wealthy foreign investors bought our banks, office buildings, industrial parks, publishing houses, hotels, and other businesses, American managements seemed bloated, and thousands of managerial employees were fired. Foreign management teams were imported to run foreign businesses here, and U.S. businesses abroad began to rely on overseas managers. When American white-collar employees went to the unemployment lines, the hotel, restaurant and rental car businesses, airlines, and other services catering to corporate expense accounts went into recession.

The real estate market collapsed as home-buying power disappeared. The Savings and Loan giveaway was the worst financial scandal in decades and the theft of billions of dollars from the public erased thousands of jobs and imperiled the entire banking system. The superwealthy class in this country grew, but the great mass of the population has lost ground faster than is commonly realized. Young people's expectations are still high, but are not to be realized. There are no new cars or houses in their future.

The average American family today cannot afford adequate medical and dental care. The dream of a college education will remain just that for many. The 1990s may well come to resemble the 1930s more than any other time in our history. As interest rates drop, the elderly are losing their interest incomes from bank savings. As the senior population grows, sheltered housing and nursing-home care is soaring to more than $40,000 a year per person.

Why U.S. Corporations Ignore Job Losses

Foreign industries fiercely defend their markets and their citizens' jobs. Why are U.S. corporations so complacent in the face of the growing export of jobs to other countries? Probably it is because of their perception of themselves as international entities. Their concern is quarterly profits and not long-term growth. It doesn't really matter to a U.S. multinational corporation where its profits come from or how they are earned. What matters is profit.

If a U.S. corporation does its business abroad, that is fine. The Chief Executive Officer will get a large bonus even if he has laid off half the company's workforce and given the jobs to near-slave laborers in Guatemala or Thailand. Foreign executives and government leaders work together in many countries to benefit their own citizens at all levels. In the U.S., our diplomats make their deals, and our CEOs make their deals without regard for each other or the welfare of the country.

Greed and selfish ambition have replaced patriotism and national feeling. Personal greed and aggrandizement have become our national policy. This has been advertised as the hallmark of good free enterprise and free trade. But no other nation shares this view. Enlightened self-interest requires a harmonious national policy and corporate policy recognizing the right of the nation to sustain its own workforce.

WE DISCOVERED THE STATE DEPARTMENT IS THE ARCHITECT OF TRADE POLICY, AND ALL AGREEMENTS MUST MEET THEIR APPROVAL.

WHY?

OUR GOVERNMENT USES TRADE FOR POLITICAL AND MILITARY PURPOSES — NOT ECONOMIC. WE ARE ALONE IN THIS PRACTICE. EVERY OTHER COUNTRY IN THE WORLD USES TRADE FOR ECONOMIC REASONS TO PRESERVE ITS INDUSTRY AND JOBS FOR ITS CITIZENS. OUR POLICY HAS MADE IT CONVENIENT FOR THE STATE DEPARTMENT TO MAKE FRIENDS BY EXPORTING OUR INDUSTRY AND JOBS.

Using Trade For Political Purposes

Our government finally gave China "Most Favored Nation" (low tariffs on their exports to us) status despite the charges of inhumane treatment of its people, employing *gulag* labor, and flaunting all our laws on safety, health, minimum wages, workmen's compensation, hours of work, etc. Why? What do we get in return?

America is now in an alarming economic decline. The world of our fathers has changed. Our manufacturing base, once the source of jobs and endless new products, is fragmented; U.S. multinational corporations are fleeing our shores; service industries once touted as the "great future for jobs" are laying off thousands of workers and are now shifting work to places like Jamaica and Bermuda for cheap labor.

Financial institutions are cutting back staffs, and for the first time since the Great Depression, thousands of white-collar, highly qualified people cannot find employment. College grads are forced to seek part-time jobs and menial tasks in fast-food places since industry offers no job opportunities. The poor in our inner cities find little employment and no hope for the future.

The outlook seems grim, jobs are scarce, our leaders insulate themselves from the needs of our citizens (President Bush refusing to increase unemployment benefits to those no longer eligible and in desperate circumstances), and foreigners now dictating our economic future. Our government has squandered our resources by blindly pursuing policies resulting in the decline of America as a world power. The root cause of our economic distress lies with these policies *and the countries which capitalized on them.*

Our People Recognize That Economic Power Is More Important Than Military Power

In 1958, America joined with other free nations in organizing the General Agreement On Trade and Tariffs (known as GATT) to ease trade between the member parties by setting up vehicles to arbitrate trade disputes and to reduce tariffs to increase commerce between its members.

One area that became a thorny issue was textiles

and apparel. This industry in America was labor intensive (requiring more labor than most products), the single largest employer in America. This source of jobs for minorities and semiskilled workers became the number one target of Far East exporting countries who had hordes of workers earning pennies an hour.

Congress prodded by U.S. manufacturers pressured the Administration to act, and The Multi-Fibre Agreement (known as the MFA) was created under GATT in 1973 to address the problem. Interestingly enough, Seth M. Bodner, then an official in the Commerce Department and later to become Executive Director of our trade association, The National Knitwear and Sportwear Association, was the architect of many aspects of the MFA. Seth Bodner today is a respected world authority on international trade.

Creating An Agreement Does Not Always Solve The Problem

Under authority granted by Congress, the Office of Trade Representative to negotiate trade agreements was created by the administration. The "marching orders" for this department supposedly were invested in developing a consensus among the government departments of Commerce, Treasury, and State. In addition, the industry "advisors" were appointed to present the industry viewpoints. I served as such for a number of years.

If an industry sector was severely impacted by imports, a complaint was lodged with the Trade Representative, and a long process began to determine if it was necessary to establish quotas on the product in question. Now the crucial element in all of this was "what were the marching orders" and who "called the shots" for the Trade Representative.

In my role as President of the National Knitwear & Sportwear Association, which represented the interests of the sweater, knit shirt, headwear, and other knitted products, it was necessary to lobby in Washington, D.C. for our industry. My introduction to the bureaucratic maze from which, supposedly, decisions were carefully made for the welfare of our citizens was most enlightening.

Our industry was "under siege" from low-cost foreign producers who had targeted sweaters as a prime target. In a few years, while Carter was in office, more than 40 percent of the domestic market was controlled by the Far East.

We pursued the Administration to meet with us to halt the import slaughter, but with no success until we launched a massive letter-writing campaign directed to Robert Strauss, then Trade Representative. He was later appointed as Ambassador to Russia by President Bush.

Strauss met with us and listened to our proposal that the government act to prevent the liquidation of our industry by limiting imports to one-third of the domestic market. He was sympathetic and assured us he would "look into our problem." At that time, the sweater industry was absorbing 50 percent of the apparel trade deficit.

Did The Import Surge Decline – No!

Foreign country after country was now shipping in sweaters with few restraints. It did not stop with our products. Other industries, shoes, electronic articles, household items, machinery of all categories, autos, trucks, motors, glass products — the list is endless — are now pouring into our markets, creating massive disruptions for industry and labor.

The import deluge was due to The Free Trade policy in effect with Carter, ballooned to gigantic proportions with Reagan, and continues with George Bush. It is a misguided plan to eliminate manufacturing in America — give it to foreigners and let America dedicate its efforts to becoming a service-oriented society.

According to our government, a service economy is supposed to give everyone better jobs, more money, and shift the dirty, polluted, low-pay jobs overseas. The unemployed factory worker knows how low the wage rates and the dead-end aspects are in the service sector.

FREE TRADE HAS BEEN REJECTED BY JAPAN, THE EUROPEAN COMMUNITY, THE ASIAN COUNTRIES AND OTHER TRADING PARTNERS. THE RESULTS CONFIRM THIS — THEY ENJOY FAT TRADE CREDIT BALANCES AND CLOSE THEIR MARKETS TO OUR PRODUCTS.

WE ARE THE ONLY NATION PRACTICING FREE TRADE.

We fought to save the knitwear industry and failed. Many other industries are struggling to survive in America today. Since the Administration would not yield or accommodate our needs, we turned to Congress for help. Under the Constitution, Congress has authority over trade policy, but abdicated this responsibility and gave the Executive branch this task. Congress retained an oversight position on trade agreements.

Congress reacted vigorously and the Special Trade Representative felt the heat. We supplied endless statistics showing how foreigners were given generous quotas and terms to ensure their U.S. market position. The trade agreements came under closer scrutiny, but the rigid policy of opening our markets to foreigners remains unchanged.

Today 75 percent of all sweaters in America are imports, and the industry is but 25 percent of its size in the early 1970s. The textile industry has been ruined and thousands of workers have lost their jobs.

Why were all efforts to get understanding and help for our position from our government fruitless?

Seth M. Bodner, the noted authority on international trade writes in his industry magazine, *The Knitting Times*, "MFN FOR CHINA?" as follows:

"Round and round we go, again deliberating about the wisdom of extending Most Favored Nation treatment to products of the so-called People's Republic of China.

"Much is at stake in this matter where the President has the authority and responsibility to consider proposing extension of MFN, and if he does, the Congress has a limited time in which to disapprove the extension.

"The tariff differences alone would be enormous, for without Most Favored Nation rates, the Peoples Republic of China would be subject to tariffs antedating virtually all modern trade negotiations and would damage their position in the U.S. market.

". . . Also at stake is the credibility of the U.S. trade laws, the posture of Congress on enforcement of those laws and of President Bush in support of fair trade and effective law enforcement.

"It is now common knowledge that the Chinese have been the source of massive transshipments (shipping goods through other countries to circumvent quotas) and are using prison labor for a variety of products exported to the U.S."

". . . One might hope that given their record the PRC's denial would be a matter beyond debate. But no. The 'let's-work-with-them-to-improve-contracts-and-make-progress-that-way' school of thought continues strong from Carter to Bush.

". . . More important, perhaps, is that this consideration of Most Favored Nation denial for the Peoples Republic of China is likely to be the last chance for both

Congress and the administration to show any serious-ness of purpose — about enforcement of trade laws."

". . . Now, with unemployment at substantial levels, with industrial and service jobs on the line as never before, now would be an excellent time to estab-lish that there is a limit and that Chinese practices have exceeded."

Recent articles in the press indicate the U.S. Attorney's office in New York is working on massive fraud by the Chinese uncovered at New York's Cus-tom House. The charge is that China has shortchanged the U.S. Treasury out of several hundred million dol-lars in the last three or four years by improperly declaring the value of goods shipped to the U.S.

Custom officials charge that big government ex-port companies are involved.

And President Bush insists on giving China the "most favored nation treatment!"

Question: Is China vital to the survival of America?

USING TRADE FOR A MILITARY REASON: At the conclusion of the Gulf War, Turkey asked for a greater share of our textile apparel market and was given it swiftly. This was a reward paid to Turkey at the expense of American industry and workers.

No regard to the prescribed procedures of con-sulting industry were observed — the State Depart-ment moved quickly to oblige Turkey.

The Wall Street Journal, April 17, 1991. Bursa, Turkey:

"Penta shipped 240,000 bathrobes to the U.S. last year under Turkey's import quota of two million. But now, in the first tangible gain, Turkey can claim from its pro-coalition stand, the U.S. is nearly doubling quotas on Turkish bathrobes and some other textile items. Mr. Akpinar, Penta's sales manager, says he will ship $7 million worth of robes to the U.S. this year, up 40 percent from last year, and hopes to double sales next year."

New York City, once the great apparel center in the U.S., now has 1,000,000 people on welfare, including many former apparel employees. Our government clearly demonstrates by giving Turkey our jobs that a very low priority is given to the job needs of Americans.

Questions Surrounding What Other Commitments Did Our Government Make To Our Gulf Allies Raised Great Concerns Among Beleaguered American Manufacturers

The U.S. Trade Representative is charged with negotiating equitable trade agreements with foreigners. Supposedly, all on behalf of American taxpayers.

From reports published in the press, the Center for Public Integrity, a watchdog group, charged that the Office of U.S. Trade Representative included in its business advisory committees paid agents of foreign companies.

The White House requested the U.S. Justice Department to rule on the legality of this policy. The U.S. Trade Representative was advised that having paid lobbyists on advisory committees was illegal. Carla Hills, Trade Representative, dismissed the foreign agents and indicated none would be appointed in the future.

Part of the trade agreement negotiating process is to ascertain the views of foreign countries affected by proposed agreements. The views of foreigners, according to the negotiating process, are factored into the thinking of our government. But foreigners should not be invited into the policy-forming discussions. This role should be relegated to the U.S. industry advisors whose role is to present the impact of such agreements on domestic industry and jobs.

*DAVID HALBERSTAM WRITING IN HIS BOOK
THE NEXT CENTURY: "PEOPLE IN
GOVERNMENT POSSESSED WITH POWER
IGNORE TRUTH. IN FACT, THEY INVENT
THEIR OWN TRUTH."*

To put into perspective all the examples of mismanagement of our trade affairs, we must know the root cause of our problem and how our relations with our trading partners accelerated the decline of our country as a world industrial power.

The decline of America as an industrial power began when our government refused to listen to its citizens and proceeded to implement trade policies based on theoretical assumptions made by people who had no experience in the real business world.

Example:

The European Community, noting the economic decline among its members, summoned the Japanese and ordered them to reduce auto shipments into their markets to pre-1989 levels. The Japanese agreed.

The U.S. auto-makers, General Motors, Ford, and Chrysler appealed to President Bush to ask the Japanese to reduce auto shipments during the recession. The public is not buying, the car-makers are suffering huge losses, and thousands of workers are being laid off. Bush rejected this appeal.

This policy astounds our trading partners who readily adjust policies to meet their economic needs.

Part of our government's thinking rests with the policy, "LET THE MARKETPLACE DETERMINE THE SURVIVOR." In other words, despite all the evidence that foreign competition operates under conditions illegal in the U.S., paying pennies-an-hour wages, employing *gulag* and child labor, subsidizing their industries, and blatantly ignoring our laws, the American manufacturer is expected to compete!

We are at the mercy of bureaucrats who never spent time in the marketplace, selling, managing people, meeting payrolls, producing, and competing head on with competition. They made theoretical assumptions creating the vast destruction of our industrial base.

As my share of the U.S. market shifted overseas, my personal experience taught me to see the Washington bureaucrats executing trade agreements were following the policy "give foreigners big quotas" with no regard for American jobs lost.

Many of my employees who had served us for over thirty years had to seek new jobs when we were forced out of business by our government's decisions. I had spent fifty years in the knitwear industry, and I have been a witness to our foolish and shortsighted economic policy, a policy that is destroying the American dream.

Look To Our Trading Partners For Answers

Our trading partners, whether they are Turkey, Brazil, or China, have an entirely different concept of doing business than we do. Foremost of these is Japan. Many books have been written, studies have been made of Japanese systems, and attempts have been made to understand why we have such feelings about Japanese inroads into the fabric of America.

One of the flaws in our thinking has been the concept that the Japanese will "come around to our ways — give them time," and so we pursue the same strategies year after year with minimal success in establishing a fair trade relationship with Japan. I feel no personal animosity toward Japanese nationals or towards Japan as a nation. I am certainly not a racist. My concern is only with the U.S. economy and threats to it. At present Japan is a major threat. In the future, the threat could come from the European Common Market or some other quarter. japan and the Japanese are highly admirable in many respects. My point is that their trade policies and ours need substantial changes.

The United States' magnanimity to a defeated enemy helped rebuild Japan industrially and gave them the tools and opportunity to replace military with economic warfare despite the national goal of Japan at one time to defeat the U.S. militarily.

Dr. Vladimir Zworykin, a former Vice-President (for life, I understand) of the Radio Corporation of America and the father of TV, related to me his visits to Japan following the war when Japan was rebuilding its industrial base for products designed for American interests. He was very high in his appraisal of their efforts to please and to produce quality products. Zworykin gave his approval for RCA to use Japan's products. Emperor Hirohito of Japan gave Zworykin the highest award given to civilians, which he displayed among his other awards in his Princeton, New Jersey, home.

The Japanese master plan for achieving world industrial domination was not apparent for many years. They proceeded methodically to select products that were the key item in hi-tech in the United States, made them for their home markets, tested consumer reaction, and studied our market for price, service, and quality. A good example of this strategy is the basic chip used in endless electronic products known as "drams." Without this chip — no production.

America dominated the world market for chips at one time. We had seven large manufacturing firms engaged in supplying domestic and international needs. Japan made its move into our market by drastically undercutting the price of drams in America.

Within a short period of time, five U.S. makers were forced out of this business.

You would think that our government would be interested in retaining hi-tech leadership (it now charges American industry as responsible) and would be able to comprehend the significance of becoming vulnerable in many key products, including exotic defense weaponry. But "let-the-marketplace-determine-the-survivor" policy was the U.S. position. The State Department is not concerned but continues to "sell Congress" that Japan is a reliable ally!

You will recall it was a Japanese company, Toshiba, who sold our restricted propeller technology to the Soviet Union.

Today Japan controls 70 percent of the world market of "computer chips" and can increase prices at will, deliver according to its terms, and dictate all purchase policies. All this action was permitted with no resistance by our government.

The Wall Street Journal, May 6, 1991:

"U.S. CLAIMS JAPANESE FIRMS WITHHOLD EQUIPMENT FROM AMERICAN CHIP MAKERS."

"A Commerce Department report says there is 'evidence' that certain Japanese companies have injured U.S. semiconductor-makers by withholding state-of-the-art processing equipment from them while providing the same technology to Japanese manufacturers.

" . . . Senator Bentsen is expected to accuse as many as seven Japanese companies . . . of refusing to sell advanced chip-making equipment to American chip manufacturers.

"Withholding technology is only one of several 'unfair trade practices' that the Commerce Department cites in its report, which addresses the health of U.S. manufacturers of chip-making equipment. The companies also face a buy-Japanese attitude in Japan, where they have to sell in order to survive, and are being 'under-priced' by their Japanese competitors in the U.S. market, the report says.

"In one key sector of the industry that produces semiconductor wafer steppers, the U.S. share of world markets skidded to 15 percent in 1989 from 60 percent in 1984, while the Japanese share soared to 74 percent from 39 percent."

One of the hazards our chip-makers face if they complain about unfair treatment from Japan are reprisals in the shape of cancellations and very late deliveries. Japan will take care of its own — not others. How unlike our government!

. . . Louis Uchitelle, writing in *The New York Times* on April 9, 1990, pointed out that a Japanese computer manufacturer might have a factory in Malaysia that makes chips and another factory in the United States that imports the chips to make a computer. But instead of being charged $10 for each chip, the price an outsider would pay, the American subsidiary shows on its books an intracompany charge of $20 . . .

What this does is to transfer profits from the U.S. back to Japan. Result: No profit in America — no taxes. The IRS is now investigating foreign-owned U.S. plants, charging we have been cheated out of billions of tax dollars.

We have absorbed about 25 percent of all of Japan's exports for years. (Source: U.S. Department of Commerce.) Japan's 1990 trade balance — we bought more from them than they purchased from us for 1990 — was listed as declining to 43 billion dollars. Not so. Not included in the total were shipments from forty-six Japanese electronic plants in Thailand. Result: Fifty-billion-dollar trade balance or 50 percent of our trade deficit is with Japan.

Since many of our economic problems concern our trade relations with Japan and since trade has many facets — understanding the Japanese strategy will bring our trade policy into sharper focus.

Scholars have attempted to establish a psychological profile on Japan. We were told that changes were taking effect and in time Japan would respond to our requests for fair play. However, reality is breaking through, and the realization is growing that Japan will not change but will pursue its master plan for economic domination of the industrial nations.

We are now advised that a commitment from Japan to rectify an inequity in our economic relationship does not mean it will correct the situation. A pledge is made *to appease us, not to fulfill its promises. The record over the past decade clearly reveals unfulfilled promises which Japan does not regard as immoral but fits their cultures.* The Japanese are now becoming very public-relations-oriented and are hiring ad agencies to improve their U.S. image. They emphasize their interests in U.S. communities, but send the profits to Tokyo.

In America, our relations with others is influenced a great deal by our laws, our inherent respect for "our neighbor's rights," and a strong desire to have others show consideration for our rights.

Our heritage has conditioned us to expect other parties to observe our moral standards, but many other nations regard us as immature. No better example exists than the trail of broken agreements, false records, substitution of products, stolen proprietary rights, and flagrant misrepresentation of facts that now exist in our trade relations with others.

Example: *The New York Times*, June 17, 1991:

"U.S. Customs reports that Honda took improper advantage of the United States-Canada free-trade agreement to avoid paying millions of dollars in duties on cars imported into the United States from its Aliston, Ontario, plant.

"The agreement stipulates *that half of the part content must come from either country. The U.S. Custom Service auditors report stated that the actual 'North American content'* of Honda Civics imported from the Ontario plant was 25 percent to 30 percent less than the amounts claimed by the company, a subsidiary of the Tokyo-based Honda Motor Company."

We Give Away Our Drug Patents

Our proprietary rights represent enormous sums invested by American pharmaceutical firms and others covering years of endeavor. China has disregarded these rights, according to news reports, and copied many of them, selling the products all over Asia at reduced prices. China stated it had a right to these patents since it was "a poor country!"

Our Friends Steal Our Products

It is reliably reported that Brazil, India, and Thailand pirate not only pharmaceuticals but also books, computer software, video cassettes, and other products that total fifty billion dollars in sales annually. Would you expect your friends and allies to steal from you?

At the current negotiations to renew the General Agreements on Tariffs and Trade in Geneva, the U.S. has insisted the protection of all proprietary rights be included and enforced among the member nations.

In regard to cars, Japan has been building assembly plants in England designed to penetrate the European market. But English regulations insist that foreign content be limited to 30 percent in each car. Obviously, this law saves jobs for the English. Why don't we have similar regulations in the United States?

In America, we have no such requirement and imported parts are as high as 70 percent. So what the Japanese have built in America are "screw driver" plants assembling cars for a greater share of the market. Since the Japanese now control 35 percent of our market, our domestic car part producers are going out of business in droves. When challenged for not buying parts from our producers, the Japanese state our quality is bad.

The history of these Japanese plants is that they were built in "sub-trade" zones which, by our government's designation, give tax and other benefits, and permit all imported parts used to be duty free!

The Japanese have cleverly exploited American discontent with past shoddy workmanship in our cars. The American consumer now refuses to buy cars with the General Motors label produced in California by a joint Toyota-GM venture. They will buy the same car with the Toyota label!

Where Have All The Jobs Gone?

The success the Japanese had in "cornering" our dram market established their master plan to broaden their control over electronic and other U.S. industries. The strategy is to move into a market by offering lower prices, service, and quality. The American supplier can't match the prices and yields his portion of the market.

As new equipment is developed by the Japanese, their home market is supplied first, giving their industry a lead over the U.S. manufacturers. Withholding these products from the American market has created severe hardships for many smaller computer and other producers. Silicon Valley, the center of our hi-tech computer sector, is held captive by these unfair trade practices.

The irony of it all is that we have been the source of all the hi-tech products which Japan is now producing. They purchased or "appropriated" our new ideas. In some cases, they were forced to pay high financial damages for their acts.

Our government has distanced itself from initiating any action to correct these trade abuses.

Japan's Interpretation Of Free Trade

Our government has charged that American producers do not try hard enough to sell to Japan. In fact, Japanese propaganda has labeled our efforts as weak, not tailored to Japan's needs.

One of our large industrial companies invented a new metal alloy that when used in energy transformers could reduce energy losses by as much as 70 percent. Japan is entirely dependent on oil imports for energy.

This technology was offered for sale to Japan. Did they buy? An old familiar pattern developed — Japan was working on their own version — and no decision was forthcoming.

As has happened in the past, a Japanese version of this new technology will appear in the market place. The Japanese home industries have capitalized on the gullible foreigners' willingness to submit new technology and to "wait for decisions" which never come. Time and again, new products submitted to the Japanese were not purchased, but in due time appeared in world markets as Japanese creations. This cloning of foreign inventions is evidence that the Japanese on their home ground throw away the rule book — as we know it.

American companies, fed up with these practices, are now pursuing Japanese violation of patent rights aggressively in the courts and are receiving huge damage awards.

How The Japanese System Works

The Liberal Democratic Party is the ruling party and has been running things in Japan since World War II. The Prime Minister, Finance Minister, and General Secretary, always "one of the old boys," are selected to carry out the policies of the small inner group of leaders of the party.

These political bureaucrats work in concert with big business and, as reported in the news, with gangsters to keep the economic engine going. This collusion closes ranks and excludes all foreigners from any worthwhile construction projects, financial undertakings, or manufacturing.

Personal relations operate independent of law. Giving of gifts to each other, clients, and employees cross all lines and are considered quite the norm by the public.

Huge financial support is given to politicians by big business and great care is given that bids for public projects are prearranged to rotate "the benefits." The power brokers develop the economic strategy for marketing products. They plan foreign investments and decide what imports to accept. They and the public frown on imports as being inferior to Japanese-made goods and encourage the maintenance of a distribution system of small retailers who are protected from foreign retail methods of buying and selling.

So effective is the system that years of pressure by the U.S. and the European Community have only made miniscule progress in getting the Japanese to buy imports.

To provide huge sums for capital expansion and

research and development, the government does not tax interest earned kept in savings institutions. This frees billions for Japanese industry to continue their huge industrial expansion with little interest to pay. Imagine the tremendous economic impact tax-free savings accounts would give to the American economy.

Ironically, our troops in Japan keep their military expenditures very low, so the Japanese have more funds to build more factories to put us out of business. Our politicians do not understand this.

In Japan, a great deal of chicanery has been exposed between large financial institutions and clients. The brokers paid back money by their biggest clients in the stock market, thus guaranteeing no losses to the largest investors.

All this is considered by Americans as corruption. The Japanese people feel it to be an accepted way of life for them.

The Japanese Master Plan To Dominate The Economy Of The U.S.

Many Japanese are emboldened by their huge success in seizing control of our industrial base and are now saying publicly or in new publications if they had known fifty years ago "how to win the war" with the United States economically, they would never have tried military power.

A great deal of analysis has been made how Japan uses its financial muscle to shape the American agenda. The plan is developed along the following lines:

One Thousand Lobbyists in the United States:

By retaining over one thousand lobbyists in America, some former administration leaders and congressional members, Japan has intimate knowledge of all pending legislation. It has effectively "watered down" pending action of Congress to redress unfair labor practices and to halt investigations into violations of our laws.

An example how far they will go is using former President Reagan to deliver their message. Of course, he was paid two million dollars to say what the Japanese want to hear. Few people seem to understand the scandal this represents — a U.S. President for hire to the Japanese.

Japanese Buy Our Research

Japan has underwritten "chairs" at many prestigious American universities. All the data developed by these schools is made available to Japan.

Japan Buys Good Will At Local Levels

To improve its "image" with Americans, it will make gifts to sundry organizations ranging from national to local centers. In fact, in my home town, the residence of Mr. Merita of Sony, our local Volunteer Fire Department sports a large new TV set — compliments of Sony.

Japan Buys Political Favors

The Japanese are now under orders to get involved in politics at all levels to show their interest in the welfare of our country. They offer to serve on committees, to raise funds, and to demonstrate they are good citizens.

At the national level, many members of Congress are "feeling the heat" when trade legislation is contemplated on the grounds that American workers, employed by Japan, might lose their jobs if restrictions are placed on Japanese products.

Japan Buys Our Communications

The Japanese now own large sectors of our publishing, movie, and TV production and have access to American thinking on an unprecedented scale. Do you think adverse Japanese publicity will be undertaken by American hirelings of these Japanese companies?

Japan Buys Our Cultural Organizations

All are funded by Japan to improve their image and in a subtle manner to get Americans to believe Japan desires to understand and to help better our relations.

TO SUMMARIZE

Here we have a foreign country with enormous financial muscle moving into the very fibre of America, employing legions of U.S. financial leaders, lawyers, corporate heads, and leading educators to carry out its programs.

The frightening aspect is our government has condoned all. *NO OTHER COUNTRY IN THE WORLD PERMITS SUCH CONTROL OVER VITAL AREAS AS DOES OUR GOVERNMENT.*

It is obvious that by blindly maintaining the "free market" policy, we have permitted a foreign nation to strip us of our heritage.

The shocking example is the response one gets from a member of Congress when he always states, "I believe in free trade" as if it were a form of life like "motherhood."

┌─────┐
│ 4 │
└─────┘

THE GLOBAL ECONOMIC WAR IS DESTROYING OUR JOB MARKET

We are in an economic war, and we have lost battle after battle. Our government has yielded ground to country after country on economic issues, and we now flounder in recessions that in many areas of the country border on the dreary depression days of the 1930s. Skilled and unskilled workers are the primary victims. They have found no political party willing to defend their interests.

Unlike the Gulf War, when trained military leaders developed strategies to overcome the enemy — and succeeded, our administration and the Congress have no plan to deal with the global economic aspects of trade and the tactics employed by our antagonists. The talk is about capital gains taxes and investment credits, both of which benefit the very rich more than anyone else.

Our approach is band-aid, and we lose each skirmish because our game plan is unrealistic. Lowering capital gains taxes will never cure our economic illness or create large numbers of jobs. Washington bureaucrats continue the same trade policies that have brought America to her knees.

Our government has created a myth surrounding its relations with our trading partners. The myth is that our partners are committed to the same free market policy espoused by our government. Being convinced of this, our Administration has persuaded Congress to accept this fantasy and the public has been fed the same nonsense.

The "party line" states that American industry has failed, that it has not been competitive, and that there would be plenty of jobs if only our manufacturers were better managers. This same false charge was made a number of times while I was involved in the trade process in Washington. When we asked the government to "show us how" to be more competitive, we were given no guidance at all.

Not in possession of the truth, the American people are fed up with our government's failure to manage our economic affairs. The public has shown its discontent and fear of the future by voting against those politicians in office. In polls taken, most Americans have given President Bush low marks for managing our economic affairs. He is criticized for performing as "Secretary of State," not as a president concerned about lost jobs, people struggling to put food on the table, and for refusing for a long time to extend unemployment benefits to those unfortunates who need extended help to survive. Eliminating millions of jobs will not produce "leaner and meaner" companies. Widespread unemployment shrinks markets.

Where does Bush live to be so unaware of the real issues demanding strong, caring leadership?

A nation of unemployed factory workers, unemployed clerical workers, and unemployed service personnel will exert a "trickle-up" effect. Eventually, widespread poverty will trickle-up to those in the highest tax brackets.

An Example Of Our Government's Thinking

The Defense Department announced it would give one billion dollars to aid Russia and then withdrew this plan after a public outcry that charity begins at home. President Bush signs foreign aid bills without hesitation and despite all reports to the contrary, he states at times that all is well in America. Who does he talk to? What are his priorities?

One political sage said plainly, "Americans vote with their pocketbooks." People demand good-paying jobs that will provide the income to live out their lives with a sense of well-being not existent at the poverty level.

Where Have All The Jobs Gone?

A Tragic Error In Policy – Trade Management Taken Over By Bureaucrats

Under the Constitution, Congress is charged with managing our trade affairs. Congress gave this authority to the Executive branch of our government during the Roosevelt Administration when Cordell Hull was Secretary of State. Cordell Hull was interested in fashioning economic ties with other nations. Once the Executive Branch was given the authority to negotiate trade agreements, our economy passed out of the hands of legislators and into the hands of bureaucrats. Trade became a "bargaining chip" for the State Department, and the result has been a disaster for America.

Common sense dictates that in war we employ generals to plan, direct and execute the military plans. In an economic war, we need generals who are experienced in business and international trade.

Trade is business, and with every country in the world fighting for a piece of our market, the battle was turned over to people in our government who developed their own trade theories with no experience in the real world of meeting payrolls, competing for markets, dealing with labor, and complicated government regulations. These bureaucrats had a disdain for business people and tolerated no requests or suggestions as to how to deal with the enemy.

My personal experience in meeting with administration officials convinced me that they were totally unsympathetic to American business and had decided to impose their theories on U.S. industry. They told the American people they could lead us to an improved economic life — all we needed to do was just accept their concept of international trade and economics.

High Tariffs Did Not Cause
The Great Depression

It is important to know that these government theorists uttered grim warnings about the dangers of "protectionism." Protectionism, they warned, would plunge America into the dark days of the depression of the 1930s. They cited high tariffs as the cause of the depression. Did you know that in the 1930s, we only imported five percent of our Gross National Product? As leading economists have pointed out, there was no basis for attributing the depression to high tariffs.

The confusion fostered by our government is that if we *demand fair trade agreements in place of our present unfair agreements, our trading partners will retaliate.*

Retaliate? How? We are the customer, and the foreigners need our market to keep their plants operating and their people employed. We absorb 25 percent of Japan's exports and 65 percent of all production of the less-developed countries. Would they antagonize the chief source of their production?

Some years ago, former Chairman of the Sub-

Committee on Trade in the House of Representatives, Charles A. Vanik, went to Taiwan and negotiated a new trade agreement on sweaters. He was able to dictate the terms and, in fact, for the first time negotiated a trade agreement that reduced sweater quotas! Vanik told me, "There was no trouble . . . he could have negotiated with any of the Asians . . . under our terms. After all, we are the customer and they need us!"

Our government wants us to believe that it would be disastrous if we demanded equitable trade agreements. But it is the responsibility of our leaders to insure that our citizens will have jobs in a global economy. We cannot permit the job market to float freely against third-world starvation wages. To do so will ultimately damage our entire economy.

Our failure to secure fair trade agreements from our trading partners has seen a hollowing out of U.S. manufacturing — the engine that provided our people with better-paying jobs. These workers are also our consumers of manufactured goods. Not a week goes by without the press reporting the signing of new trade agreements **with foreigners, all tailored for the benefit of others – better diplomatic relations or to help retailers, but not our workers.**

The Wall Street Journal, October 8, 1991:

"A policy change by the Commerce Department has infuriated some entrepreneurs who contend that it could hurt their business.

"The row stems from Commerce Department rulings that so far have slashed duties imposed on certain Chinese manufacturers by changing the government's method for determining whether such manufacturers are selling goods in the U.S. at artificially low prices.

"Companies such as Consolidated International

Automotive, Inc., Los Angeles, are alarmed. If the decision stands, it 'will eventually wipe out' the 60-employee company, asserts Mark Plumer, its owner.

"The producer of automotive lug-nuts last Friday filed a lawsuit against the U.S. agency with the U.S. Court of International Trade. The suit accused the Commerce Department of using 'unlawful' methods in determining what antidumping duties to impose on a Chinese lug-nut competitor. Under the new method, the duty was 4.24 percent — sharply below the 66.49 percent level under the prior period.

"With only a four-percent duty, Chinese manufacturers can produce lug-nuts, which are used to attach wheels to automobiles, at less than Consolidated's cost of material, Mr. Plumer contends."

This action by our Commerce Department is an example of how our government neglects the welfare of our citizens. The American economy is founded on small business. Small business employs more people, creates additional new jobs and products, and pays greater taxes than does big business.

Who are our government officials working for? The changed world economy requires changes in U.S. policies if we are to participate in the new world market.

A Look At How The European Community Manages Trade And Prepares For One Free Trade Zone In 1992

The twelve nations comprising the European Community, Belgium, Britain, Denmark, France, Germany, Greece, Ireland, Italy, Luxembourg, Netherlands, Portugal, and Spain have united to form the largest and most integrated common market in the world. Over the centuries, many of the members have been involved in bloody conflicts between themselves extending into decades. Their individual cultures are distinctly different, and nationalism is a fervent aspect of their political outlook. Yet they have agreed to a common currency and will work closely together.

The economic need to survive has dictated the decision to give top priority to develop free trade relations between the member nations to enable them to compete against the Japanese and American inroads into their markets. They recognize the need to *prepare for the mounting challenge by foreigners to their industrial sector and are willing to submit to a plan that will aid survival of jobs and industry.*

The European Free Trade Association (EFTA) member countries involved are Austria, Finland, Iceland, Liechtenstein, Norway, Sweden, and Switzerland. This bloc has expressed a desire to coordinate trade efforts with the European Common Market. This would create a market of nearly 400 million consumers, dwarfing all others in the world.

As reported in the press, this new, expanded market would operate as follows:

Products and services would move freely throughout Western Europe unhindered by duties, taxes, and quotas.

Workers would be able to exploit the job market throughout the 19 countries. All academic and professional degrees would be recognized throughout the market.

Programs to rectify pollution and sources of damage to the environment would be organized.

Farmers would continue to maintain their own existing policies.

A European Council of Ministers would be set up to deal with disputes.

Financing would be made available with low-cost loans to the poorer member nations.

In All Of The Planning, Concerns For The Survival Of Small Business And Jobs For Labor Were Addressed. "Let's Make SureThe Spanish Plumber Keeps His Job" Is The Attitude.

The Europeans' concept of free trade is to accept it within limitations. A new import agreement was concluded with Japanese auto-makers for the '90s. The first report hailed the agreement as giving Japan a greater increase of the Common Market. But the agreement specifically lists as imports, cars produced in Japanese plants in England. It also limits imports that would disrupt the markets of auto-manufacturers in Italy, Spain, and France. If conditions deteriorate in Europe, then imports would be reduced accordingly. In reality, the entire sales increase would then come from newly built Japanese car assembly plants in Europe, not from Japan.

London auto analysts questioned regarding this new auto agreement did not feel it would open The Common Market to any further expansion of the Japanese portion of their market. They called the new plan "Protectionism."

Do you think the Europeans consider this a violation of the free market policy? They acted realistically to keep their industrial engines running to provide strong economies. This is good business judgment.

If our government were to exercise the same approach in dealing with Japan, what do you think would happen to the most basic job engine in America — our auto industry?

When the Eastern European countries recently began discussing ways to get access to the rich Western European market, the French objected. The French argued that low-cost East European products, particularly foodstuffs, would lower the incomes of French farmers. The result was that the East European countries were denied access to the European markets.

Former Prime Minister Edith Cresson of France has openly attacked the Japanese closed-door policy and defines it as "hermetically sealed." She pointed out how the Japanese are wiping out the U.S. auto industry, and she did not want hundreds of thousands of jobs to disappear. Former Prime Minister Cresson has also expressed the fear that Japan would overrun Europe's computer chip industry (as America permitted Japan to do). She is quoted as saying that the Japanese have a strategy of conquest and that they would like to devour Europe.

The French vigorously deny that their position violates the free trade concept.

The Europeans were quick to recognize the danger of Japanese predatory pricing when the Japanese took over the American computer chip market. To prevent American-style economic surrender, the Europeans instituted regulations that only chips "printed" locally would have free access to the Common Market. Fujitsu of Japan then announced it would build a large chip-making operation in England!

The Europeans have subsidized the commercial aircraft Airbus company for 21 years. During this time, they have spent 26 billion dollars for its operation. Involved are England, France, Germany, and Spain. Despite huge operating losses, the Airbus Company continues its business and has taken away 15 percent of our own McDonnell Douglas sales. McDonnell Douglas has now been reduced to only 15 percent of the market.

Airbus now controls close to 40 percent of the world market, challenging Boeing's position as the leading world supplier of commercial aircraft. Airbus has loaned aircraft "free of charge" and offered easy terms and low prices to persuade U.S. airlines to purchase Airbus equipment. Airbus can't fail. The Europeans are determined to take a big piece away from one of the few remaining industries in the U.S. with a worldwide market. Boeing can't match the terms of Airbus.

When the U.S. protested the massive subsidizing of Airbus, the Europeans said bluntly that they would not let their civilian aviation industry be dismantled.

U.S. Government Response:
Let The Marketplace
Determine The Survivor

McDonnell Douglas recently planned to sell 40 percent of its stock for 2 billion dollars. The proposed sale was forced upon the company by its loss of market share and a shortage of capital. The buyer was Taiwan Aerospace, a newly formed company that has never built an airplane part. For the first time, this deal would give foreigners access to technology we have restricted from sale for years.

If this deal is allowed to stand by our government, we will in effect have invited vast Asian capital involvement in an essential American company. McDonnell Douglas is the nation's largest military contractor, making the F15, F/A-18 fighters, helicopters, and other vital military hardware.

Carla A. Hills, the United States Representative, was reported at a meeting in Tokyo to have commented that foreign investment in a company like McDonnell Douglas is a logical extension of the kind of manufacturing alliances that have arisen in the last decade.

Congressional responses to the proposed sale differ — Senator Jeff Bingamon, Democrat of New Mexico, is reported to have said that he would seek to block such a deal if it was judged harmful to American interests.

Representative Richard A. Gephardt, the House Majority Leader, is reported to have called the negotiations a very negative development for the United States and amounts to a giveaway of American technology.

Want To Open A Factory In Russia? – See Federal Agency, The Overseas Private Investment Corporation

You will have to buy a plant in Russia, then receive insurance coverage from the U.S. Federal Agency against expropriation, political violence, and currency convertibility problems. *If you want help in America against losses from foreign* invasion of your market — do not apply!

Negotiations to renew the General Agreement on Tariffs and Trade have been under negotiation in Europe for many months. The United States wishes the Europeans to reduce the large subsidies given to European farmers. In addition, the U.S. is attempting to reduce all imports tariffs on foreign-made textile apparel products.

Our government has classified apparel *as a protected industry! Currently every country in the world with a sewing machine is exporting into our markets. Imports control 65 percent of the U.S. market, and thousands of our semiskilled workers have lost their jobs.*

As an example, New York, once the provider of manufacturing jobs for minorities, newcomers, and the vast numbers of workers who do not or will probably never qualify for the sophisticated hi-tech jobs, has seen a loss of 700,000 manufacturing jobs since 1950 and 150,000 in the 1980s during the so-called "golden years."

The Europeans are not about to give up their farm subsidy programs, and negotiations to renew GATT are stalled. One of their demands is that we cancel the U.S. Trade Act, which under Section 301, gives the president the authority to institute trade sanctions for unfair practices against the offending country. This is the only recourse American producers have to stem the flood of illegal foreign goods shipped into our markets. Unfortunately for our workers, the president is very loath to act and wants to "maintain good relations" with the offending countries. Congress, under our Constitution, must approve the GATT agreement.

Europeans Act To Save
Their Electronics Industry

The European Common Market now shows an annual trade deficit of 40 billion dollars in electronics. The Europeans are now fully aware of the inroads made in their market by foreigners. *They have also taken particular note of what happened to America's consumer electronics industry now dominated by foreigners.* The European community is marshaling all its forces to rebuild its electronic sector and correct the mistakes of the past.

The European arms-makers share the views of the Pentagon and say it would be unwise to depend on Japanese chip-makers. They might get squeezed into a shortage, or the Japanese may jack up the prices.

Some of the following programs are being initiated in Europe to strengthen their electronics industry.

Research is being financed by the Community as part of this effort.

Small companies are urged to merge to strengthen their operations.

France has taken the lead by providing $700 million in capital to state-owned Groupe Bull, and an additional $400 million for research. Moreover, broadcast rules have been changed to help European producers compete with the next generation of TV sets.

Companies in different European countries are being urged to cooperate with each other by pooling research funds and the like.

European companies are encouraged to try to solve their problems without surrendering themselves to Japanese or foreign arms-manufacturers. Britain's largest computer-maker, International Computers, Ltd. is an example of what not to do when they sold out to Fujitsu, Japan's largest computer-maker. The Europeans are acting to prevent selling out to foreigners.

The [EEC] has contributed more than $500 million for research on new generations of computer chips by a consortium called The Joint European Submicron Silicon . . .

. . . There are also government-backed research projects on data transmission and computer-aided manufacturing . . .

. . . the community [has] rejected Japan's broadcasting standard for high definition or HGTV . . . Brussels adopted a European standard.

(Source: *The New York Times,* September 4, 1991.)

The European Community has recognized the threat to its economic survival and adopted coordinated measures to "get back into the ball game."

Some action has been taken in America to reestablish its lead in semiconductor technology. This effort is coordinated by Sematech, a 14-company consortium of large computer manufacturers, with a $200 million annual budget, a modest sum when compared to the European Community programs. From reports in the news media, it appears that the Administration officials are divided over the role of government in preserving our hi-tech industries. The decline of these key industries has been the result of government policy. It would appear that the Administration officials now aware of the problem would act to save these industries.

Common sense dictates that government must act as the catalyst to revitalize industries that are vital to the nation's welfare.

Government Policy: Let Industry Solve Its Own Policy

Who created the problem that saw five of our seven computer chip-makers forced out of business by Japanese predatory acts? The president's advisors, if employed in the business sector, would have been fired long ago for their poor performance in watching over the public interest.

The Europeans are taking active measures to protect jobs. Unfortunately, America has not been served well by Congress or the Administration in watching over our job market. It is not enough for the government to protect corporate profits. It must also respond to our overall economic needs, especially the loss of decent jobs for millions of Americans.

On export subsidies: The United Kingdom subsidizes 35 percent it exports, Japan 35 percent, France 29 percent, Germany 12 percent, and the U.S. six percent.

(Source: U.S. Controller General.)

The less-developed countries exports: The U.S. absorbs 64 percent, the European Community 25 percent, and Japan three percent.

Asia: The Next Major Trading Block

Asia: The Next Era Of Growth

Since the vast changes in Western Europe with the collapse of communism and America's concentration of its diplomatic efforts centering in Europe and the Mid-East, Asians are now developing their own plans for their economic future.

Japan has been most active in financing new manufacturing facilities in Southeast Asia. The rising cost of manufacturing in Japan and the keen competition from other Asians have provoked Japan into shifting marginal profit products to Asian countries where workers are paid less. There are now 46 Japanese electronic plants in Malaysia, for example.

The shifting of manufacturing into such areas has been the practice of American multinational corporations for years. Motorola is reported to have built 13 plants in nine nations, and General Electric is reported to have the largest manufacturing facilities in Singapore. Our open market policy encouraged shifting these jobs to Asian countries. Products manufactured there are shipped back to America with few restraints. Although our workers have lost their jobs, they are urged to buy these foreign products.

The Four Tigers, as Hong Kong, South Korea, Singapore, and Taiwan are called, have been industrializing for years. They enjoy large credit balances of trade and, in the case of Taiwan, are now using their vast dollar reserves to invest capital abroad.

The six nations of Southeast Asia (Brunei, Indonesia, Malaysia, the Philippines, Singapore, and Thailand) are pooling their capital, labor, and raw materials. They are also lowering transportation costs, which gives them access to new sources of raw materials. Their activities are generating investment capital so that they can maintain steady industrial growth abroad as U.S. industry shrinks.

The chief shortage in the Asian countries is engineering and technical talent. Japan is providing technicians to close this gap. However, the shadow of a warlike Japan still hangs over this region, and Southeast Asians are reluctant to accept Japanese technical dominance. The Southeast Asians are, in fact, taking steps to protect themselves from the Japanese.

The expansion plans by some of the members of this Asian trading bloc are very impressive. Taiwan will spend over $300 billion during the next six years to improve her infrastructure. Hong Kong plans to spend $16 billion for a new airport and is reported to be planning a new superhighway into southern China for easier access to sources of manufacturing.

China's Exports To The U.S.

Some 2500 Taiwanese companies have invested $3 billion dollars in China's Fujian Province during the past six years. For years, Hong Kong has used plants in southern China to manufacture an array of products labeled and shipped "Made in Hong Kong." One estimate is that the economic output of Greater China will exceed that of France by the year 2000. The United States regards China as a totalitarian dictatorship which has massacred citizens advocating democracy.

The Asians have made investments in themselves that exceed any new investments from the U.S. It is estimated that the Asian gross domestic product, excluding Japan, will reach $5 trillion by the year 2000, rivaling the European Community and almost equal to that of the U.S.

Up until 1990, American companies invested $46 billion in this region. The U.S. economic decline has slowed our influence over Asian plans. They are asking for an American presence but primarily because of uneasiness over Japan's intense drive to dominate the economy of East Asia. Trade has increased with America dramatically, and the Asians, including China, are enjoying huge credit trade balances.

Japanese exports to this region will reach $107 billion this year compared with $60 billion from the U.S. Japanese investments will reach an estimated $8.7 billion, the U.S. $4.4 billion.

Investment Abroad Is Good For Investors

It is reported how American companies such as Coca-Cola, IBM, Motorola, Hewlett Packard, Du-Pont, Proctor & Gamble, and Apple Computer are all actively expanding their operations in East Asia. Motorola has a $400 million complex in Hong Kong and is expanding into Asia's telecon and semiconductor markets.

This is good news for the American economy in terms of gross national product. It is good news to our economists in Washington, D.C., to investors and stockholders. But foreign investments and profits do not create jobs at home. There is little benefit to the average American wage-earner.

In the opinion of many observers, the Asians do not feel it necessary to observe American proprietary rights and laws. The Chinese, Malaysians, and Taiwanese have demonstrated openly their total disregard for many American pharmaceutical patents and have copied and distributed these pirated versions throughout Asia at discounted prices. This disregard for our patent rights extends into other product lines. Some of the violators have stated that, as poor nations, they have a "right" to appropriate our inventions.

Where products are on quotas issued to various countries, the Asians transship, sending excess production to neighboring countries to have labels changed and sent into our markets under a legitimate quota. For example, Chinese-manufactured ski jackets were discovered bearing labels, "Made in Macao."

Our customs officials are unable to inspect the millions of shipments pouring into our ports of entry daily. Knowing this, the foreigners mislabel the shipments. If quotas are filled on pants, they will change the overshipments designating a category such as socks or jackets that has an unfilled quota.

It is very common for the Asians to test overshipping a product into an American port of entry that has limited manpower, knowing it unlikely will be caught. If the initial shipment passes, future shipments are sent to that customs port of entry.

Hungry for hard currency, the Asians have a policy of subsidizing their manufacturers, enabling them to sell their goods below cost. For years, the sweater industry in America has complained to our trade officials of this violation of our laws. Finally, desperate for relief, the U.S. sweater industry litigated the countries of Hong Kong, South Korea, and Taiwan before the International Trade Commission and proved that the Asians were "dumping" or selling merchandise below cost. American companies won the case after paying enormous legal fees. According to our laws, both buyers and sellers are liable, and as a result, substantial penalties were ordered by the ITC. This suit was only a temporary inconvenience to the Asians.

Cheap Chinese Labor Eliminates Jobs For Americans

With a population of over one billion people, representing almost one-quarter of the globe, the emergence of China as an industrial power has far-reaching impact on the economies of the rest of the nations on planet Earth.

Although 75 percent of its work force is engaged in agriculture, the remaining 25 percent available for other industries have proven to be productive and quick to adapt to Western methods of producing goods.

For many years, the province of Guangzhou, bordering Hong Kong, has been supplying export products for sale in Hong Kong. The exports are sold bearing the label "Made in Hong Kong." China originally accepted this arrangement as a way of evading U.S. restrictions on trade with a hostile state. A form of capitalism flourishes in Canton unlike other provinces in China, and this promotes exports.

Reports have circulated for some time of child labor in China. Children are said to work as much as 70 hours a week, living in barracks, and paid pennies an hour. A recent news media report estimated that 500,000 prison laborers are employed in factories making products destined for the U.S. market. The use of prison labor for these exports is strictly forbidden by U.S. law. However, Chinese exporters lie about the origin of these goods. There are no governmental regulations for Chinese manufacturers to observe. The government needs hard currency and will sell products at prices no Western country can match. The Chinese use exporters based in Hong Kong.

Countries attempting to sell to China are finding the price for doing business is high. Car dealers must give two cars of each model to the government "free" and pay huge sums to have their products "tested." Since the government must approve all imports, tariffs and trade barriers are high, creating limited sales opportunities. Foreign businesses cannot thrive in China. No similar restrictions are placed on the Chinese exports to the U.S., however. Giving the Chinese communists a large share of our jobs will make true friends of them in the eyes of our State Department.

China Is Given Easy Access To Our Markets

China welcomes foreign capital investments in its southern provinces. Ironically, capitalism flourishes in this region with the blessing of the Chinese rulers. Enterprising Chinese businessmen own expensive cars, have nice homes, and possess all the latest hi-tech conveniences made available through neighboring Hong Kong.

The city of Shenzhen has numerous factories established by American companies. These factories produce thousands of shiploads of toys, shoes, and clothing — all destined for the U.S. market. The "lean Christmas sales" the past few years reflects the reduced American consumer buying power. It is remarkable that our economists who favor free trade cannot comprehend that unemployed workers limit their purchases to the bare essentials to maintain their lives.

So when Congress prepared to vote on cutting off trade to punish the Chinese government, lobbyists for U.S. retailers, toy sellers, wheat farmers, and technology companies descended on Capital Hill armed with startling numbers: $15.2 billion worth of "Made in China" goods were sold to U.S. businesses last year. That included 40 percent of all toys and 38 percent of all shoes sold in the U.S. in 1990. It should come as no surprise that the U.S. unemployment lines are lengthening.

Lobbying under the banner of the Business Coalition for China Trade were leading American companies, many listed in *Fortune 500*, giants who have blanketed Capital Hill, urging Congress not to lift Most Favored Nation treatment for China. Joining in was the U.S. Chamber of Commerce. Missing from this lobbying effort were those most affected by the low-cost Chinese imports — our unemployed workers who had seen their jobs exported to China.

Imports from China have been growing at a rate of 27 percent a year.

China is behind Japan as the chief exporter to America. We absorb one-third of China's exports. As a result, American manufacturers have been able to close plants and lay-off workers, while they turn to import cheaper goods.

WHERE WERE THE LOBBYISTS FOR THE MIL-
LIONS OF AMERICAN WORKERS WHO HAVE LOST
THEIR JOBS TO CHINESE IMPORTS AND THE
THOUSANDS OF AMERICAN MANUFACTURERS
FORCED TO CLOSE THEIR FACTORIES BY NOT
BEING ABLE TO COMPETE WITH THE LOW WAGES
OF CHINA'S MILLIONS OF WORKERS?

*OUR GOVERNMENT HAS NO INDUSTRIAL
POLICY. "LET-THE-MARKETPLACE-DETER-
MINE-THE-SURVIVOR" THINKING HAS
BROUGHT AMERICA TO ITS INDUSTRIAL
DECLINE. POLITICIANS ARE NOT CAPABLE
OF DEALING WITH THE PROBLEM OF EVEN-
HANDED TRADE RELATIONS WITH THE NA-
TIONS OF THE WORLD.*

A real danger to American manufacturers is the
political unrest of the jobless. David Duke and others
like him may take this opportunity to attack American minorities, and the whole social and political
system. The outcome of rebellion by the unemployed is not predictable, but it is very likely that the
whole country, including corporate importers will
suffer. Lack of foresight may cost American diplomats their jobs.

Taiwan Takes U.S. Jobs

This island country of about 20 million people
has developed into a major exporter of electronic
products, apparel of all categories, machinery, tools,
jewelry, supplies for apparel-makers, plastics, hardware, auto supplies, professional tools, and many
products used in the construction industry. Taiwan
Trade Associations sent me a number of catalogs, and
the list of products they offer is mind-boggling. And all
this occurred during the past twenty years.

Taiwan serves as a major contractor for many of the world's largest companies, chiefly American. In the early stages of industrialization, apparel was the chief export. Taiwan quickly expanded into electronics after observing the Japanese success in this area.

Look at the labels, and you will see that "Made in Taiwan" is on countless products shipped freely into our markets.

To accommodate the great demand for its products created in part by a vast network of agents throughout the world, Taiwan turned for cheap labor to mainland China. The Peoples Republic of China, despite its public refusal to accept Taiwan as an independent nation, gazed elsewhere as Taiwanese capitalists used mainland China's factories for its needs.

Taiwan May Buy The United States

Taiwan today has dollar reserves greater than the U.S. Treasury. It enjoyed a trade balance of $12 billion in 1990 and today is now exporting capital into America and other parts of the world.

Taiwan capitalists have expanded production to become one of the world's major semiconductor producers in less than ten years. But overexpansion has created severe market problems for this industry.

Taiwan has restricted imports of many categories for years to shield its domestic industry and protect its own profits and jobs. After much pressure from the U.S., it is slowly opening its markets to some of our products.

We Support South Korea's
Invasion Of Our Job Market

South Korea was created after the Korean Conflict and was soon the beneficiary of vast economic aid from the U.S. With a population of about 40 million people hungry for employment, South Korea quickly became a chief source of cheap apparel for American retailers. Large American chain stores established buying offices in South Korea, and the apparel invasion of America began. This has grown into mammoth proportions — all aided by generous quotas given to South Korea by our government.

South Korea is a fierce competitor of Japan. Korea imitated Japanese strategies for exploiting world markets for key items. This is seen by the Koreans as a stepping stone to achieve control of foreign industry and markets.

South Korea expanded into manufacturing electronic goods, steel, ships, autos, and a host of other products — all produced at prices the American manufacturer could not meet.

Some years ago, the President of the Japanese Knitwear Association met with me to seek advice. What was the problem? South Korea's cheap prices, he said, are putting Japanese sweater companies out of business!

South Korea always imported freely from the U.S. until 1990. Recently, it established controls on imports to improve its trade balance. The Korean worker receives much lower pay than the American worker. But as the U.S. job market collapses, we may soon have a large pool of desperate workers who will gladly accept a job for minimum wage and less.

South Korea's Version Of Free Trade

For years, South Korea enjoyed a substantial balance of trade with the U.S., but when rising labor costs and greater competition from Southeast Asian competitors resulted in a trade deficit of $1 billion with the U.S. in 1990, South Korea swiftly introduced measures to reduce imports.

It raised tariffs and taxes on American-made

products to make import costs on "luxury items" prohibitive. For example, ordinary dried garden peas were classified as "luxury" items! In the past, fresh food shipments required only five days to clear Korean Customs but were now delayed for months. Result: Spoiled shipments, unacceptable.

Consumer items were delayed to be "tested." It was reported cosmetics were held up for many months under this new system. If you wanted to buy a refrigerator selling for about $1600 in the U.S., it would cost over $4000 in Korea. These restrictive measures reduced American imports to a fraction of the $13 billion exported into that market in 1989.

The South Koreans repeated their commitment to free trade and denied that their actions closed their markets to our products. They had learned from the Japanese how to keep domestic industry and jobs for their citizens.

The Far-East Version Of Free Trade

South Korea is not alone in closing its markets to our products. We see an organized policy of restraining imports by all the Far-East nations trading with the U.S. The foreigners tailor their trade policy to maintain stable manufacturing facilities at home in order to insure a strong domestic economy.

These nations have organized the Asia Pacific Economic Cooperation with the purpose of bonding themselves into a common effort. The development in Western Europe in 1992 of a single trading bloc has triggered the unity of the Pacific nations to look inwardly for economic growth.

Japan is the role model for many of the emerging industrial countries in this region. Its closed-market trade policy has many adherents. Taiwan and China enjoy large trade balances but have a stingy import policy.

Our government pleads with the Japanese, Chinese, and Taiwanese to open their markets to our products. Japan agrees "to study the problem" and appoints committees to make recommendations. Nothing happens. We continue to retreat behind a passive policy of hoping Japan will change and open its markets to us.

New Japanese Prime Minister
Warns U.S. Congress

In taking office as the next Prime Minister in Japan, Kiichi Miyazawe is quoted as delivering a stern warning against protectionist sentiment in the U.S. Congress! This is an outrage since Japan has the strongest protectionist policies of any nation. However, Japan is beginning to negotiate from a position of strength, and Japan's arrogance is becoming steadily more obvious.

THE AMERICAN GOVERNMENT FANTASY: A YUKON-TO-YUCATAN FREE MARKET

As a response to the emerging two major trading blocs, the European Community and the developing Asian bloc, our government has proclaimed after establishing a free trade agreement with Canada that we should conclude a free trade agreement with Mexico. The result would create new markets for American goods — so states our government.

This trumpet call repeats the same message used after free trade agreements were concluded with Japan and the European Community. These agreements resulted in exporting 12 million American high-paying manufacturing jobs over the last decade. Our trading partners enjoyed a $100 billion trade balance last year while our debt to others has reached over $700 billion dollars. As to new jobs created, the millions of American workers, desperate to find work, could rightfully ask WHERE ARE THE JOBS?

With American industry limping along seeking to survive in a domestic market crowded with foreign-made goods, it was reported that President Bush moved beyond the North American free trade zone concept and signed a pact to relax trade barriers with the four South American nations Brazil, Argentina, Paraguay, and Uruguay.

If our leaders were forced to face the unemployment lines, would they continue the same trade policies they now cling to?

The Canadian Free Trade Agreement

Are the Canadians happy with the free trade agreement?

This agreement took effect in early 1989. Trade barriers were reduced on a number of products and what appeared to be a "good deal" for the Canadians turned out to be a big headache that has the Canadian government reeling.

Canadian manufacturers are now pouring across the border by the hundreds attracted by **lower U.S. wages, lower taxes, and real estate**. They are setting up plants in the United States and closing their operations in Canada.

The Canadian Labor Congress, representing Canada's trade unions are greatly concerned over the economic dislocation created by the free trade agreement. The decline in their industry, some of their economists point out, compares to the sharp decline our Midwest is experiencing with the shifting of auto manufacturing to cheap labor in Mexico.

Our Midwest has not recovered from the loss of manufacturing, and the shortage of higher-paying jobs has created enormous economic problems for the Americans in that region.

As for the free trade pact with Canada, the free access to the Canadian market for U.S. companies, relieved of substantial tariffs and other regulations, has made it possible to set up subsidiaries to capture a larger share of the Canadian market. Canada's major foreign investor is the United States with Japan increasing its holdings at a rapid pace.

Canada, in providing substantial medical and other benefits to its people, in excess of that in America, has increased the tax burden Canadian business must carry. The cost of Canadian manufacturing has reduced its competitiveness. For example, as was pointed out by Stephen Van Houten, president of the Canadian Manufacturers Association, the Canadian wage in 1990 had risen to about $12.97 an hour as compared to the American Wage of $11.10 per hour.

Canadian Consumers Make Pocketbook Decisions

Canadians had done their cross-border shopping in the U.S. for years, but now this activity has accelerated rising 19 percent in one year. American cigarettes, food, liquor, clothing, and electronic devices of all categories are less expensive than in Canada. The weekly savings from shopping in America is estimated to total about 20 percent of an average Canadian household budget.

The news media has featured the huge traffic of Canadian shoppers pouring into our border states and returning with cars loaded with supplies of all categories. When the Canadian shoppers were questioned if they felt guilty spending their funds in the U.S., the answer was, "we can save a lot of money — and that's all that counts with us."

It is estimated that as much as $2 billion dollars are spent a year in the U.S. by the Canadian cross-border shoppers.

Canadian Businesses Decline Under The Free Trade Agreement

The Canadian retailers are furious and worried. Sales are declining and profits shrinking, creating a high mortality rate among Canadian businesses. Failure to be competitive with U.S. producers is linked to the cost of high welfare, health benefits, and high wages in Canada. All these benefits coupled with higher taxes have added to the cost of their products.

We enjoy good relations with Canada — but —

Despite the free trade agreement, the Canadians attach conditions to trade designed to close their markets and protect domestic industry. Our plywood products were rejected by Canadians on the grounds of "poor quality!"

For years, Canada had stringent license requirements that excluded American grain products. Recent relaxed rules still require an end-use certificate from the Canadian Grain Commission stipulating that the grain must be used at the facility to which it is sent. The U.S. does not impose any curbs on grain imports from Canada.

Canada enjoyed a favorable trade balance of over $8 billion with the U.S. in 1990. The Canadians protect domestic industry in negotiating trade agreements.

We visited Canada in the summer of 1991 and found the Canadians angry and depressed over the free trade agreement with the U.S. They wanted no part of it!

The Free Trade Agreement With Mexico

The free trade agreement contemplated by our government with Mexico poses enormous consequences for the future of manufacturing in the U.S. Since the engine that creates jobs, higher income, and economic power is manufacturing, the question raised is what benefits will our citizens have from such an agreement?

Our State Department and members of the Executive branch, including President Bush, are touting free trade as the medicine to cure our economic woes. They are oblivious to the greatest concern our citizens have as we begin to adjust to the "lean '90s" as the next decade is called.

Americans are worried about finding and keeping their jobs!

The shifting of jobs overseas and to Mexico has so weakened our "job engines" that any further decline will create economic and social chaos in America. No glib assurances about future economic benefits are going to convince Americans about the benefits of a free trade agreement with Mexico unless they experience the same job opportunities in America their parents had. Based on the steady decline in manufacturing in America, these jobs are not materializing unless we change our trade policies and the people who manage them.

Looking At Mexico

The Wall Street Journal, Monday, April 8, 1991:

Mexico has a population of 85 million people, of which 50 percent are below the age of eighteen. Mexico has a 2000-mile common border with the U.S. Agriculture accounts for 50 percent of the National Product and employs one-half of the work force.

The large Mexican birth rate adds about one million workers a year, mostly children who enter the work force at the age of 12 although it is illegal to hire children under 14. The Mexican authorities estimate that five to ten million children are employed illegally, very often at hazardous jobs. "Economic necessity is stronger than a theoretical prohibition," says Alfredo Farit Rodriguez, Mexico's Attorney General in Defense of Labor, a kind of workers' ombudsman.

The above article describes how poverty forces young children to quit school and become engaged in manufacturing products that are hazardous to their health. As an example, in the manufacture of shoes, the glue used contains toluene, a petroleum extract linked to liver, lung, and central nervous system damage. Many workers develop chronic illness working in this environment.

Living conditions in Mexico are primitive with as many as 25 people living in a two-room home. As many as eight children are forced to share the same bed. Working for low wages has locked the working Mexican family into poverty.

What became of our government's position on human rights?

Mexico And The Environment

Currently, 25 percent of fruits and vegetables consumed in America annually are imported from Mexico. The lack of enforceable regulations governing the use of pesticides by Mexican farmers is raising great concern among our health authorities. Our growers must adhere to regulations restricting use of chemicals that affect the environment and the health of our public. There are no health controls covering the rising shipments of Mexican foodstuffs to the U.S., now totaling over $1 billion annually.

The Rio Grande River and the Nogales Wash bordering our two countries are the most polluted rivers in the world. Toxic waste and untreated sewage pour into these waters creating enormous health problems for both the U.S. and Mexico.

The American manufacturing plants that now number in the hundreds on the Mexican border operate with no antipollution equipment, creating severe environmental conditions. The contamination of these waters, a source of drinking supply for Mexican and U.S. border states is revealed in a report from the state of Arizona that the incidence of hepatitis in Arizona has increased 20 times the national average.

California has placed environmental regulations

on various industries, such as furniture-making and metal-plating. These shops moved across the border and now operate in Tijuana, Mexico, producing toxic wastes from their use of solvents. Enforcement of Mexican environmental regulations is nonexistent.

By going to Mexico, the American producers have chosen the easy and more profitable path in making their products. The free trade policy encourages these producers to move operations to Mexico, exploit cheap labor, give few benefits to the Mexican workers, and ship the end products back to the U.S. These manufacturers pay small duties and escape any allegiance to our country's needs.

The exporting of American jobs continues with the blessing of our government.

The lack of pollution controls is illustrated at Nuevo Laredo, Mexico, opposite Laredo, Texas, which dumps about 25 million gallons of untreated sewage into the Rio Grande River each day, making it impossible for the recreational use of that water.

The 1.2 million residents in Ciudad Juarez, Mexico, across the Rio Grande from Laredo, Texas, use firewood for cooking and heating fuel. Rubber tires are burned in kilns that make decorative bricks and tiles. Along with pollution from motor vehicles and industry, the smoke from these fires produces an acrid cloud over both cities in certain weather.

The lack of sanitary facilities in the homes of many working Mexicans poses enormous health problems. As the number of plants continue to increase in that region, the impact their operations have on the environment and the health of the workers living in that area pose problems that the Mexican government lacks resources to rectify.

How does our government, made sensitive to environmental considerations in America, deal with the negative impact of no environmental controls in Mexico?

Want A Job In Mexico?
Earn $27 For 49 Hours

The wage rate for the "maquilladora" (workers in semiskilled border plants) factory worker in Mexico is $27 for a 49-hour week. If he has more experience he can earn about $47 a week. The Mexican auto assembly worker earn considerably more averaging about $3.00 an hour. By comparison, the U.S. auto-assembly worker earns from $14 to $15 an hour.

The result of this wide difference in wages has seen a shifting of U.S. auto and truck production into Mexico. We are faced with overproduction of cars and trucks in America when one factors in the imports from Japan, which now control 35 percent of our market.

General Motors announced a drastic reduction of producing cars and trucks in the U.S. and Canada over the next two years. Twenty-one of GM's 125 assembly plants will close down, affecting 18 percent or 70,000 jobs.

General Motors is reported to employ 55,000 workers in Mexico. Will these low paid workers be laid off?

Agriculture In Mexico?

The wage rate paid a Mexican farmhand is about $4.00 to $5.00 a day. The migrant farmhand in the U.S. is paid the federal minimum wage of $4.25 an hour. In addition, all American employers pay a host of benefits, unemployment insurance, social security, health and hospitalization, pension, and other benefits — all necessary for the welfare of our citizens.

Free Trade With Mexico And
How Foreigners Benefit

With the Mexican free trade agreement now under discussion, many foreigners, Asian and European, are eyeing the Mexico pact as another opportunity to set up manufacturing operations in a cheap-labor environment. They are ready to seize the opportunity to ship more of their products into the U.S. market free of duty and quotas. President Salinas of Mexico was quoted as encouraging foreigners to take advantage of these opportunities.

Nissan Motor Company of Japan is reportedly planning a $1 billion auto assembly plant in Mexico — all designed to ship in cars and trucks to the U.S. duty free. Despite the American auto companies cut back in operations, laying off thousands of American workers because of the inroads made by foreigners in our auto markets, Nissan and others are pressing ahead to capture more of our auto market.

Volkswagen, Germany, is already established in Mexico. The free trade agreement would enable Volkswagen to enlarge its U.S. market share substantially. For our domestic auto producers, the "pie gets smaller and smaller."

Asian Apparel-Makers Go To Mexico

Apparel-makers from Asia seen an opportunity to seize an even greater share of the American market and have established plants in Mexico to take advantage of no quotas. The U.S. apparel industry, weakened by 65 percent foreign domination of all apparel sold in America, will have difficulty surviving in the next decade. What will the millions of semiskilled apparel workers look forward to but welfare and poverty?

U.S. Food Processors Look
South Of The Border

Attracted by the low Mexican wages, American food companies have begun shifting their operations there and sending the packaged food north. California, with an $18 billion agricultural industry grows half of the fruit and vegetables Americans eat, is most heavily involved in this transferring of operations to Mexico.

The current drought and the increasing pressure by state and federal authorities to provide adequate housing for the migrant workers employed to harvest the crops made the wages paid in Mexico for farm work from $5.00 to $8.00 a day impossible to resist. Towns like Irapuato, north of Mexico City, and More- lia in Michoacan, west of Irapuato, became the homes for large U.S. packing plants processing tons of veg- etables daily — all destined for the American market.

Thousands of American jobs in food processing plants paying as high as $9.00 an hour in California and elsewhere in the West are now exported to Mexico. California is losing its appeal as a source of better- paying jobs.

What does it take to make our government understand that it has created the current economic crisis in our economy?

Multinational U.S. Corporations Think Global, Not American

U.S. manufacturers have been established in Mex- ico for years; DuPont, General Motors, Ford Motors, AT&T, SCI Systems, Campbell Soups, Chrysler, Kim- berly-Clark — to name some. General Motors is reported to employ 55,000 workers in Mexico. U.S. multinational manufacturers think in terms of being global — not American. They practice no allegiance to America nor care for the future of our country. Corporate leaders think for "the short term," receive large salaries, bo- nuses, and huge retirement benefits. The stockhold- ers' rights are ignored, and corporate heads, by their own selfish aims, destroy the company loyalty that was characteristic of the American personnel in the past.

There are now an estimated 2,000 American plants now established in Mexico. An estimated 500,000 workers are now involved in the producing of products destined to be shipped into our markets. Using the established formula that for every direct manufacturing job lost, 2.5 others engaged in supplying machines, parts, raw materials, and services are also lost, we could state that 2,250,000 American jobs were shipped to Mexico.

THIS IS WHERE SOME OF THE AMERICAN JOBS HAVE GONE.

FROM THE VANTAGE POINT OF THE AMERICAN WORKER, THE MEXICAN FREE TRADE AGREEMENT IS NOT WORTH THE PRICE.

SUMMARY

For decades, our country has been sponsoring a trade concept that has created economic distress for millions of Americans. In contrast, the Europeans and the Asians *use trade to further their economies. Our government uses trade for political and military purposes.* It is this policy that fosters recession, plant closing, cut-backs in personnel, budget deficits, poverty, huge deficits at all state and local levels due to reduced industrial activity, and the decline of America as a world economic power.

Washington bureaucrats, secure in office term after term, have no knowledge of the emotional trauma people experience in losing a job. Many of our young have not experienced a recessional environment where no jobs are available for college grads or factory workers. The number of management personnel unable to find work has reached the greatest number since the Great Depression.

Sections of our country, New England and the Midwest, describe economic conditions in depression terms. All the so-called growth period of the Reagan years have been revealed as the greatest mismanagement of public funds in the history our country. The Savings and Loan scandal is symptomatic of the decay that writers like Paul Kennedy, noted Yale historian, writes of in his book, *The Rise And Fall Of The Great Powers* (Random House.)

Where did it begin and why is it so difficult for our leaders to accept the reality that the responsibility of our industrial decline is theirs?

Trade creates or destroys jobs. It depends on the deals made.

At the outset, we should define what trade is. Trade is business — pure and simple. To be successful in business, you must know your market, be able to produce what is needed at the right price, and service your customer.

Trade is WAR — AND YOU MUST HAVE THE RIGHT PEOPLE AND POLICIES TO WIN SUCH A WAR. To win the Gulf War, we organized a strong team of military leaders, gave them the tools, and *the authority to make the decisions*. This is the way to win a war. Our elected officials lack the skills to carry on an economic war.

The government's position in regard to the free trade agreement with Mexico has the same elements that has seen us lose battle after battle for jobs in this country. They use flowery phrases how "our destinies are linked," etc. Do you think that Mexico or Japan think in these terms?

In every economic plan, we should ask the question — will the American people benefit? It not, discard the plan.

There will be and should exist trade relations between nations. What is missing in our policies *is the inability of the Washington bureaucrats to relate to the results of their discussions when they conclude trade agreements.*

Too many economists and theorists in Washington, D.C. have dominated the policy-making too long in America. The American people, now living in great economic distress, know this, and all polls point to the great disillusionment the public has with our political leaders.

The Washington bureaucrats have insulated themselves from events that destroy the fabric of the lives of our people. They do not possess the credentials to carry out the necessary reforms to save America for Americans.

IF OUR GOVERNMENT CONCLUDES A FREE TRADE AGREEMENT WITH MEXICO WITHOUT USING THE CRITERIA OUR TRADING PARTNERS USE, THE REMAINING MANUFACTURING SECTOR IN AMERICA WILL BE SUCKED INTO THE CHEAP-LABOR MARKET OF MEXICO. IT WILL BE CATASTROPHIC FOR AMERICAN WORKERS AND OUR ECONOMY.

We need to create a strong Industrial Policy Board to shape and manage the business of trade. This body appointed from the business community, with long experience in international trade, should function *independent of the political system.*

We have a role model in The Federal Reserve Board which for many years has managed our monetary affairs independent of the political system.

The global economic war we are exposed to demands radical action if we are to survive as an industrial power.

PRESCRIPTION FOR REVIVING INDUSTRY IN AMERICA

"Leadership is the ability to get men to do the things they don't want to do and to get them to like it."
President Harry S. Truman

The Global Trade War has engulfed the U.S., and our government is without a plan or a course of action to meet the challenge. The country yearns for some leaders with knowledge of business methods and the experience to execute practical plans to revive America's declining industrial base.

Wanted This Kind Of Leadership!

During the Great Depression, President Roosevelt recognized that fear possessed the American public. He addressed this emotion and proceeded to initiate action to rebuild new hope for Americans by initiating bold steps to change the economy of the nation.

When war with the Nazis loomed as inevitable, President Roosevelt structured agencies to manage the war effort. The War Production Board, created to marshal all production of the country, was placed in the hands of members from the business community.

He did not place such responsibility in the hands of Washington bureaucrats. The results of this common sense decision are well detailed in history. American civilian needs were met as well as those of the military. The United States industrial might spelled defeat of the Nazis.

ADOPT NEW POLICIES AND SELECT NEW PEOPLE TO SAVE AMERICA FROM BECOMING A THIRD-CLASS WORLD POWER

WE SHOULD CREATE *AN INDUSTRIAL POLICY BOARD* EMPOWERED TO INITIATE ACTION TO RESTORE AMERICA TO ITS WORLD INDUSTRIAL LEADERSHIP. THIS BOARD IS TO *OPERATE* INDEPENDENTLY OF THE POLITICAL SYSTEM.

A new concept? In 1913, the Congress created the Federal Reserve Board, which has managed our monetary affairs *independently of the political system.* What chaos would exist if we left the management of our money system in the hands of the Washington bureaucrats whose ineptness in management has created billions of dollars of losses in our savings and loan and banking system. Not to mention the personal extravagances these same officials practice — all at the taxpayers expense.

Proposed Structure of
THE INDUSTRIAL POLICY BOARD

• Members of this Board to be (12) individuals selected from industry, with long experience in the business world and international trade. The members of this Board would be empowered and committed to reviving our American manufacturing industry. Appointments to this Board would be made by the President with the advice and consent of the Senate.

• Terms of office would be three years. Board appointments would be staggered to maintain experienced members.

• Compensation would match that paid by industry to attract the best talent.

Role of THE INDUSTRIAL POLICY BOARD

PRIORITY NO. 1

• All authority to negotiate trade agreements would be given to this Board. To avoid interagency conflicts and to promote a unified trade policy with government, departments currently involved in the trade process would relinquish this authority to the new Board. Currently, the State, Commerce, Treasury, and Defense Departments are engaged at one time or another in the trade process. Transferring such authority to a Board whose membership *is not beholden to political pressure and to members of industry grasping for special considerations would accelerate the rebuilding of our economic power.*

PRIORITY NO. 2

• The new Board would examine the trade policies of our trading partners, particularly Japan and the European Community. The cornerstone for business survival is to know why the competition is successful. THE INDUSTRIAL POLICY BOARD would move swiftly to shape our policy patterned after the trading policies of our trading partners.

THE EUROPEAN SYSTEM

The current economic policy of the European Community is revealed in that 60 percent of all trade is confined inside the Community. Once the process of creating "one market" is accomplished, this figure may well rise to 70 percent.

The message is quite clear. The Europeans are committed to the policy of *retaining their manufacturing base regardless of GATT or any other agreements to which they render lip-service.* They call this action common sense. Our government calls it protectionism. We lose the jobs and our partners thrive.

Our government's inability to admit failure and its stubborn adherence to ill-advised and destructive foreign trade policies makes it amply clear that decisions involving trade cannot be made by American politicians. The deep recessions we experience plainly indicate politicians are not business people *and foreign trade is business.*

The Asian countries, under the leadership of Japan, are referred to as the Greater Asia Co-Prosperity Sphere. Japan, by making huge investments in this area, is now dictating economic policy. The Asians recognized the strategy of the EEC and have adopted their own policy of keeping trade contained within their membership. *Over 60 percent of all Asian trade is confined to Asian countries themselves. They see the decline of industrial America and are building their own economic power base.*

THE INDUSTRIAL POLICY BOARD faced with the reality of the Global Trade War could structure its response to meet this challenge.

PRIORITY NO. 3

THE INDUSTRIAL POLICY BOARD would identify American industries essential to the welfare of the U.S. It would establish mechanisms to insure that the U.S. manufacturing sector be revived to supply the basic needs of our citizens and our military.

Because we have lost control of our own vital industries, during the Gulf War 17 of the 19 exotic weapon systems used by our military needed foreign parts to operate. During World War II, we manufactured 95 percent of all the parts needed for our weapons. The 20th century has seen amazing technological changes. *We were able to create the amazing advanced technology used in the Gulf War, but poor management by our government saw this technology shifted to foreign manufacturers.*

THE INDUSTRIAL POLICY BOARD, acting as did the War Production Board *during World War II,* would identify those industries deemed necessary for the revitalization of our industrial base. Regulations would be initiated to expand these manufacturing facilities and to organize with the aid of existing government bureaus the financial and technical assistance required.

Is this the "fearful protectionist policy" our government has declared will create the loss of jobs and the decline of America? What does our government think has happened the past 20 years when U.S. free trade policy destroyed the mightiest industrial machine in the world and exported 12 million manufacturing jobs, depriving millions of our citizens of secure, high-paying jobs?

By What Formula Could
All This Be Achieved?

To revive old plants and create new manufacturing facilities will require swift, strong measures. The formula for this approach is now in place, created (hard as it is to believe) by our government when it limited foreign imports of steel to 20 percent of our markets. Our Defense Department saw that foreigners were "dumping steel" into our market and that the American producers were on the verge of failing. The Defense Department demanded "protection" for the U.S. steel industry and got it! Our steel industry, secure with 80 percent of our market, modernized, became more efficient, and can now compete in all world markets.

When manufacturers are secure of their market share, they will be more inclined to invest in American plants and reduce shifting their operations offshore.

And this is not all. Our government has two standards — one for the manufacturers and one for the farmers. The peanut and sugar cane growers are protected from low-cost imports, but the manufacturers are left to fend for themselves in a fierce competitive global market.

Unbelievable as it sounds, the Bush Administration now wants to remove the 20-percent limitation for foreign steel and give foreigners complete access to our markets!

Carla Hills, U.S. Trade Representative, has stated that $1 billion in U.S. exports creates 20,000 American jobs. *If that is so, then $1 billion in imports eliminates 20,000 jobs. With a trade deficit of $100 billion, using her formula, we lost 2,000,000 jobs in 1991!*

The Industrial Policy Board
And "Market Sharing"

Our trading partners factor in their planning *which portion of their markets they wish to maintain to provide jobs and economic security for their citizens.* We must learn from them.

The rebuilding of production facilities in the U.S. should meet the following criteria: 1) The product manufactured is essential for the security of America. 2) The product is necessary to provide jobs for Americans who do not or many never qualify for hi-tech positions. 3) The plants are needed to preserve our fair share of the U.S. market.

During World War II, the War Production Board compiled a list of essential industries to maintain the needs of the war effort and our civilian population. By establishing input with industry associations, data from government agencies such as the U.S. Department of Commerce, U.S. Treasury, the Department of Defense and academic America, the *INDUSTRIAL POLICY BOARD* could introduce plans to rebuild American industry.

For example, some years ago we were the largest world supplier of computer chips. WE INVENTED THIS TECHNOLOGY. Computer chips are used in countless electronic products, and their availability determines the production capabilities of many products *and determines the success of new products.*

The demise of the computer chip industry is well known. Under "free trade," the Japanese copied our technology, flooded our market with computer chips at very low prices, and forced five of the seven of our large producers out of business. Our electronic industry is now at the mercy of the Japanese computer chip industry. Production of new American products are delayed or abandoned for lack of parts. Remember the old nursery rhyme "for want of a nail, the shoe was lost — then the kingdom?"

MARKET SHARING would correct this vulner-ability. Manufacturers in America would have confi-dence to invest in America, to build plants creating higher-paying jobs for our citizens. What manufac-turers need is the assurance that low-cost foreign pro-ducers would not be permitted to flood our markets.

Our government has tossed out statistics in an attempt to prove that the American consumer benefits from low-cost foreign products. However, the studies made by Congressional committees, industry, and unions have revealed that the retailer buying cheap imports *does not actually pass on the savings to the con-sumer, but uses a higher markup in most cases.* The re-tailer purchasing an import sweater for $4.00 will sell it as high as $16.00, using a 400-percent markup on cost. On domestic goods, the markup is about 100 percent, so that a sweater purchased for $8.00 sells for $16.00.

Many other products offered by American retail-ers do not pass on to our consumers the huge cost savings from cheap foreign labor. The American re-tailer importing a shoe from China for $5.00 does not pass this low-cost saving on to the American con-sumer. China, notorious for its disregard for our laws, now ships 74,430,000 pairs of shoes annually into our market. China has crushed all attempts at democracy, yet as a cruel repressive dictatorship, its products are welcomed here.

The countless products now manufactured by U.S. manufacturers in foreign countries at cheap prices and shipped back for sale in America do not reflect savings to the U.S. consumer.

We Can Provide Jobs For American Labor

About 80 percent of our workforce lacks ad-vanced technical skills required for jobs in hi-tech industries or the skills needed for jobs in our financial service centers. Semiskilled workers provided the labor for industries like apparel, shoes, autos, and endless factory products basic to American life. The jobs have now been given to foreign workers.

"Market Sharing" will create a "ripple effect" reviving suppliers and the service sector, which depends on manufacturing. Once our "job engines" are restored to former strength, they will create the higher-paying jobs denied our workers these past decades.

The Sweater Industry Can Provide 150,000 New Jobs

In dealing with the Washington bureaucrats regarding imports that overwhelmed the domestic sweater industry, we recommended that 35 percent of our market be allocated to imports. This would leave 65 percent of the U.S. market for domestic producers. This policy would take people off the welfare rolls and continue to supply work for millions of semiskilled workers, many of whom are women and minorities. The Washington bureaucrats rejected this plan on the grounds that free trade was the only way to go.

If *THE INDUSTRIAL POLICY BOARD* were to institute "a market share policy" as practiced by the European Common Market, and the import level of sweaters was limited to 35 percent of the domestic market, the impact on this one industry would be dramatic.

The total number of *direct new jobs that would be created would be 50,000. The service industries supplying raw materials, machinery, parts, factory supplies, and services would total 100,000 jobs! The result would see 150,000 new jobs created.*

(Source: Seth M. Bodner, Executive Director, National Knitwear & Sportwear Association.)

The American Shoe Industry Can
Provide 500,000 New Jobs

The American shoe industry share of the U.S. market is now only 13 percent. (Source: U.S. Department of Commerce.) If the American shoe industry was given 65 percent of the domestic market, over 275,000 new, direct American job opportunities would be made available. Factoring in the service industries, *an additional 500,000 jobs would be created.*

The Beleaguered Auto Industry Can
Provide 375,000 New Jobs

Currently, the Japanese ship 1.7 million cars into our market, eliminating the jobs of 250,000 Americans employed in direct manufacturing jobs. Employing the same "market sharing policy" and giving Japan one million cars annually in our market, we would add 125,000 new auto production jobs. Adding in the additional support jobs required, *a total of 375,000 new jobs would be injected into a faltering, much-needed basic industry.*

The Apparel Industry Can
Provide 720,000 New Jobs

The American apparel industry currently employs one million workers. Imports dominate 60 percent of the U.S. market. The number of jobs lost in this labor intensive industry totals 240,000 since 1980. Exercising the same formula of "market sharing" and giving foreigners 40 percent of the U.S. market, *a total of 720,000 new jobs would be created in this vital industry.*

Apparel manufacturing has been the source of jobs for minorities and new citizens in America for generations. The loss of jobs for these workers, who do not qualify for hi-tech jobs, can result in an increase in the welfare rolls of many U.S. cities, particularly New York.

The government has reported that we export over $2 billion of apparel annually. Not so. Included in this statistic is cut fabric sent to other countries *to be returned to America as finished apparel! The true total of apparel exports is about $600,000.*

If the current plan of our government to eliminate tariffs on textiles and apparel is adopted at the GATT negotiations, imports will rise to over 80 percent of the U.S. market. This will create additional losses in textile and apparel of more than one million jobs for Americans according to Wharton.

What is astounding is to read that our government calls the apparel industry "a protected industry!"

(Source: Dr. Herman Starobin, Director of Research, International Ladies Garment Workers Union.)

Many industries would benefit from an intelligent "market sharing" policy. The economic benefits to millions of Americans would change the social structure of our country. Steady employment with higher compensation would shift people from unemployment and welfare into productive tax-paying citizens.

Our young could look forward to achieving the rebirth of the "Great American dream" denied them these past twenty years. All this is a far cry from working at wages barely above the minimum wage in the service sector. Our youth is being denied some of the basics their parents were able to experience. We can change all this if we are not afraid to recognize the cause of our problem and act on it.

Multinationals, Their Leaders, And Global Trade

The habits developed by overpaid American industrialists, who give themselves fat bonuses and many other benefits regardless of whether their company makes a profit, will have to change under the leadership of *THE INDUSTRIAL POLICY BOARD*. These corporate leaders do not identify with America, but think only in terms of profits.

Foreign-Based Companies Rejoice At U.S. Free Trade Policies

Many U.S. multinational corporations are quick to support U.S. free trade policies. They have abandoned U.S. workers in order to profit from the flaws in the free trade policy. To them, free trade means an opportunity to expand abroad and ship back into America products manufactured by impoverished foreign laborers forced to work for pennies a day. Of the Fortune "500" corporations, 150 make all their profits outside the U.S. They engage in exploitation of foreign laborers as bad as anything practiced in the days of robber barons.

Foreign-affiliated companies have accounted for an ever-rising share of the merchandise trade deficit. This trade deficit reached 78 percent in 1989. Part of the problem is that U.S. owned foreign-based corporations tend to purchase plants and equipment from abroad, not from American sources.

(Source: U.S. Department of Commerce.)

A foreign-owned subsidiary in the U.S. pays lower taxes than U.S. owned competitors.

U.S. Corporate Giants Lay Off U.S. Workers And Hire Foreigners

When General Motors announced it was cutting back 75,000 workers due to plant closings, it failed to mention the 55,000 workers employed in Mexico who are paid a fraction of their American counterparts. When IBM, as reported in the press, announced massive layoffs, what of the divisions operating abroad? Or did General Electric, reported to be the largest manufacturer in Singapore, announce cutbacks there reducing its personnel?

Foreign Citizens Save On Taxes In The U.S.

Want to pay fewer taxes? Establish an American subsidiary. Foreigners do so for greater profits for their home-based operations.

Residents of Japan, with investments in this country, pay a tax rate here of 6.1 percent. Americans with incomes between $40,000 to $50,000 pay 11.6 percent in taxes in the U.S.

How is all this possible? Our government, ever mindful to "take good care of our foreign relations," continues the same illogical approach to global trade. Give the foreigners special treatment so that our State Department can maintain cordial relations.

Foreign subsidiaries in the U.S. are provided with parts, supplies, and services by the parent company. The foreign parent company sets up billing procedures charging very high rates for all these services. For example, if a part costs $5, the American subsidiary is charged $10, creating a smaller profit on which it would pay about 30 percent in taxes.

The parent company with a very high markup on all services and parts to the U.S. subsidiary enjoys a far greater profit and pays at a much lower tax rate than if the profit were realized in America.

Government investigations reveal that the practice of foreigners to shift profits from the U.S. to the parent company abroad is long-standing. This unchecked violation of our laws has resulted in the loss of billions of dollars in tax revenue.

The global economy that economists hail as the way of the future needs to operate *with controls. It must not be left in the hands of corporations who have demonstrated a total disregard for the country that gave birth to their operations.*

THE INDUSTRIAL POLICY BOARD COULD "PLUG THE HOLES" IN OUR SYSTEM THAT PERMITS PRODUCTS MANUFACTURED IN LOW-WAGE COUNTRIES TO FLOW UNCHECKED INTO OUR MARKET. FRANCE RECENTLY DEMANDED THAT THE EUROPEAN COMMUNITY RESTRAIN SHIPMENTS OF POLISH HAMS INTO FRANCE AT PRICES DETRIMENTAL TO ITS FARMERS. THE HAMS WERE NOT SHIPPED INTO FRANCE.

How The European Community Practices Free Trade

For four years, members of the General Agreement on Tariffs and Trade have been negotiating a renewal of this agreement.

The Europeans have built into their system a large subsidy program for their farmers and a massive financial subsidy program for their Airbus Company, builder of aircraft to compete with Boeing in the U.S. and in the world markets. When asked to discontinue this unfair competition, the Europeans state flatly they intend to maintain their subsidy programs. Airbus is now undercutting Boeing in all markets, offering low prices and generous credits. The U.S. does not give any such aid to our aircraft producers.

The Europeans are committed to preserve jobs

for their people. At this writing, the future of GATT is uncertain.

Needed: A National Industrial Policy Board

The success of restructuring our industrial base will require broad participation by labor, industry, the academic world, and the government. *THE INDUSTRIAL POLICY BOARD CAN FOSTER THE AMERICAN VERSION OF JAPAN'S "KEIRETSU."*

Japan's "Keiretsu" system is a joint effort by the financial, industry, labor, and government sectors to maintain a unified industrial policy. This has been the key to Japan's huge economic success.

THE INDUSTRIAL POLICY BOARD, acting as the "coach and manager" could fashion a national effort of all U.S. industry sectors to join with U.S. labor, educators, and financial centers to function as a team in resolving industrial problems. Congress would be asked to modify existing laws to remove barriers between this form of cooperation.

To Survive In Business: Learn From Your Competition

American companies are now moving to incorporate in their planning the Keiretsu system. Reports describe how over 250 research and development consortia have been established, designed to pool their research in new technology. As an example, the Big Three U.S. auto manufacturers are working together on a new battery for an electric car. In a rare instance of understanding its role in the Global Trade War, the federal government contributed $120 million for this endeavor.

Again, learning from the success of the Japanese system to make the suppliers contribute the engineering and the creation of new systems, American firms are now forging alliances with their key suppliers to aid in insuring that needed products meet the product requirements *in advance of the manufacturing stage.*

To achieve full cooperation, large companies are now limiting the number of their suppliers and giving large commitments to achieve prompt delivery, top quality, and reasonable prices. The results in cost savings and profitability have been startling to the U.S. companies whose policy in the past was to "play one supplier against the other." This policy has reduced the number of suppliers in many industries, reflecting how competition produces casualties.

The U.S. producers now find that equity investing in strategic suppliers is a form of insurance. New products flow to the investor and the cost of research and development is now shifting to the suppliers for many new products.

Strangely, large companies are now marketing competitors' products, something unheard of a decade ago.

The New York Times, January 1, 1992:

"WILL THE UNITED STATES LOSE ITS EDGE IN WORLD MARKETS IF IT IGNORES THE GLOBALIZATION OF TECHNOLOGY?"

". . . Since, as is widely acknowledged, American industry often lags behind foreign companies in manufacturing, the nation's competitive edge now depends on being able to create new technologies faster than overseas rivals . . ."

". . . Among the policy issues is whether the government should try to stem the overseas migration of American technology by such measures as blocking acquisitions of key American technology by foreign corporations . . ."

". . . [Clyde] Prestowitz is in the camp of strategists

and policy-makers who argue that the globalization of technology, can still be, and should be, held in check. . . . It is far more difficult, for instance, for an American company to buy a Japanese one than vice versa, they note, arguing that the United States would be naive not to look out for its own interests . . ." (Clyde Prestowitz is president of the Economic Strategy Institute in Washington, D.C.)

". . . We're the only country in the world that thinks nationality doesn't matter, said Pat Choate, an economist who is a leading critic of foreign investment in the United States . . ."

Role Of Education In Industrial Order Creating Job Engine Opportunities For The Future

At one of my lectures at Ramapo College in New Jersey, the Chairman of the International Trade Department, Dr. Joseph Le May, made an interesting observation.

"Academic America," he stated, "has failed to prepare its students for a role in manufacturing. Too much emphasis in the school curriculum has been placed on the staff functions service in the corporate area."

At the next meeting of the International Advisory Board of the college, Dr. Le May included in the agenda the question of introducing the subject of manufacturing in the school curriculum!

The recession in America is making parents aware of the inadequacy of today's college degree as a solid entry into the modern workplace. Families and students are demanding a better-organized curriculum and faculty more tuned into today's economy.

My own experience has been that academic America is reaching out into the business world for people to lecture their students on "life in the trenches" — as working for a living is called.

A recent press article reported a poll of the nation's top 25 business schools revealing that graduate students are now rediscovering industry. For the 1991-1992 academic year, 83 percent of the schools are adding manufacturing courses to the curriculum. This is up from 43 percent five years ago.

In addition, 61 percent now offer a manufacturing operations major compared to 48 percent five years ago. At 83 percent of the schools, student enrollment in manufacturing courses has increased for five years.

The Wall Street Journal reported that Stanford University receives a $3 million gift from the Sloan Foundation in New York to help create a doctoral degree in manufacturing. It aims to grant 50 such Ph.D.s in a decade.

The greatest service our educators could perform is to review some of the educational measures used by Germany and Japan in preparing their students for the future. The era of the fast buck is gone. The chips are down, and a retraining of some of our educators to the real world is mandatory. Included in this process is the responsibility of the parents to join in the new effort to make education relate to the needs of the marketplace.

If we rebuild our manufacturing sector, there will be a need for students to serve as interns in preparation for future participation in industry. The Germans have had an apprentice training system for over a 100 years. The quality of their products reflect the great importance attached to training their youth how to make things well.

Americans could learn from this sound approach.

From time to time, the news media departs from its customary role of reporting the crimes, the violence, and the pain we humans inflict on our neighbors. A refreshing report describes how Eli Broad, a charitable businessman raised in Detroit, felt strongly about the decline of this region and made a $20 million gift to Michigan State University to its business school. "We need brighter people to go into manufacturing," Mr. Broad is quoted as saying!

The New York Times, July 21, 1991:

President Bush's announcement of the formation of a private foundation to help create "a new generation" of American schools has some people wondering whether the Administration is expecting the private sector to pick up the tab for its education reform proposal "America 2000."

The foundation was set up at the behest of Mr. Bush to persuade corporations to contribute as much as $200 million to create 535 experimental schools intended to be models of reform.

Educators and state and local officials complain that they were not included in the planning for the foundation, though an advisory committee of educators has been added as an afterthought.

Critics say that the plan falls woefully short considering the 80,000 public schools in the U.S. A massive effort would be required to meet the plan's goals.

The corporate sector has not embraced the plan wholeheartedly, pointing out that it was an unconscionable burden on corporate resources.

Many corporations have donated direct and indirect support to public elementary and secondary schools. There are 140,000 business school partnerships, ranging from local programs to major efforts at the state levels.

Some business leaders say they are concerned with what they see as arm-twisting from the administration to contribute to the foundation. In addition, many want to know why some of the money cannot come from existing corporate support.

Manufacturing Belongs In School Curriculum And Career Planning

• Introduce the magic of creating things to our young. There are many sectors in manufacturing covering electronics, telecommunications, fiber optics, laser technology, electrical systems, apparel-making, shoes, microwaves, cameras, tile-making, furniture, steel, auto, and a host of others which must be studied and understood in school.

• Introduce the employee skills industry requires.

• Outline the various roles at the supervisory and higher management levels industry seeks in its staff personnel.

• Study the techniques introduced by Japan on the manufacturing floor, which are now trickling down in the thinking of many American plant managers.

• Outline contemporary production techniques as a prelude to new manufacturing dynamism for the next decade.

• Review and introduce the QUALITY IMPERATIVE as preached by the pioneers of quality control, Americans W. Edwards Deming and J. M. Juran. Japan seized and introduced the Deming quality control precepts 40 years ago and made his teachings synonymous with Japanese products.

• Develop an intern arrangement with local industry for students to learn "on the floor" how products are made.

• Establish a close partnership with corporate America so that the school curriculum is tailored to industry needs.

• Realistically develop the economic future possible for students making manufacturing their majors.

At one time, this country had many specially funded public agricultural high schools. These schools combined academic courses with agricultural science to prepare a nation of farmers for jobs. The idea of introducing manufacturing to high schools is in this long-established tradition.

Many members of academic America have "written off" the mundane tasks performed in manufacturing and have stressed that America's future lies in the "added-on-value" approach. This means teaching should stress that increasing the desirability of a product is most important. This concept stresses introducing management, engineering, and development of new hi-tech products as the role for the future.

Unfortunately, only 20 percent of our work-force qualifies for these jobs, and it will require a vast effort to increase that percentage. This school of thought suggests we leave the making of products to other nations with cheap labor. But our unskilled labor force needs jobs and must have jobs. The alternative is unrest, crime, riots, and revolution.

This "added-on-value" approach must be accepted as *part of the solution to our industrial problem. But we must deal with a workforce* that is not and may never be in a position to meet this criteria. We need to plan for the welfare of all Americans who comprise our workforce. The jobs for these people can be made available.

Introducing manufacturing at the high school level could open up a vast new workforce for a revitalized U.S. industry. Those students, with talent, could continue the advanced courses colleges would offer in manufacturing.

FILLING THIS ROLE IN OUR ACADEMIC SECTOR WOULD ADD TO THE POWER AND SUCCESS OF THE EFFORTS TO REBUILD AMERICAN INDUSTRY.

In our educational system, in the fields of math, sciences and physics, the grades of our students have fallen behind other industrial countries. The consensus is that a joint partnership between parent and teacher and a new review of teaching techniques could be the catalyst for improvement.

Role Of Labor In Rebuilding Industrial America

Our current labor force has inherited the work philosophy of the past generation. My experience in manufacturing was built on the accepted concept that production was paramount and quality an added ingredient.

"Planned obsolescence" was the standard maintained by many of our large corporations. If the product wore out quickly, the consumer purchased a new one. I recall my auto dealer calling me every two years advising me to trade in my car — or else I could look forward to mounting repair problems.

This philosophy worked fine for years. People were busy making products, earning nice wages, buying homes, sometimes a country place, two cars in the garage, extra TV sets, and sending the kids to college.

You received an annual bonus, had a medical plan, saved money for retirement, and even subsidized the children when they married and started their own homes. All this was the lifestyle during the 1950s and into the 1970s. The consumer griped about shoddy workmanship in his car, household appliances, and the careless attitude the service area exhibited toward complaints. Not much changed until — the fat, juicy American consumer market, filled with discontented Americans caught the fancy of the Japanese.

The Japanese capitalized on the sloppy attitude of our producers and supplied the American consumer *with quality at a cheap price. The Japanese did not make money initially. They wanted our market and proceeded to eliminate the fat-cat American manufacturers from product line after product line.*

The rest of the Japanese invasion plan to dominate our economy is well known by every high school student. Only during the last five years has there been a reawakening among American producers that the game plan is changed and survival calls for an overhaul of our production system.

The U.S. worker is now asked to change his work habits — or else — no jobs. The re-education of the people in the workplace must be developed in an orderly manner. The Japanese plants in America have be-come role models in developing good relations with personnel to improve quality and production. *It has been clearly demonstrated in these Japanese plants in America that given the right leadership and a working partnership role our factory workers can match the quality and performance of the Japanese and the Germans.*

This generation of labor will have to discard the old mass-production concept which stressed quantity over quality in the products made. *If we are going to survive as a world industrial power, labor will have to face up to the grim reality that maintaining quality must be the paramount concern in the attitude toward the job.*

U.S. management has created the policy resulting in the decline of quality and service in the products offered the American consumer. Obsession with short-term profits, no long-range commitment to product development, and greed for personal gain have dominated corporate thinking too long. If labor is expected to change, then the leadership must show the way. It is encouraging to see that the new crop of industry leaders has heard the message and is now providing the tools for change.

Labor can and will cooperate, but the commitment must be permanent. There is "no quick fix" to cure America of the sins of the past. If the worker is to perform more efficiently, companies will have to invest more in training. Too much effort on the part of companies was directed toward managers, technicians, and professionals, not rank-and-file workers.

As a result, fully 89 percent of American workers never receive any formal training from their employers. We can correct this mistake and train our workers.

What Of The Role Of The Unions?

The power of unions in America has been in decline the past decade. The new factory worker seems more content dealing with management directly, unlike his father who experienced the need for a united front to achieve worker benefits.

The adversarial relationship between unions and management in the U.S. is long-standing. The competition to "get the best deal" created strains and economic distress for all parties. The union leaders saw the huge benefits enjoyed by corporate leaders, even if the company lost money, and wanted some of the benefits also. If we are to achieve the "new order" in manufacturing, the adversarial environment between unions and management must change to one of cooperation. A partnership must be formed — again using the Deming approach, adopted by the Japanese as a role model. Only through a commitment to create a common ground for labor and management in which to operate can we survive industrially.

Role Of Industry Under The Leadership Of The Industrial Policy Board

IT IS NOW ESTIMATED THAT 70 PERCENT OF MANUFACTURERS IN AMERICA ARE EXPOSED TO INTERNATIONAL COMPETITION.

The multinational corporations in America pose the greatest problem for restructuring our manufacturing base. During the past decades, they have been shifting part of their operations overseas. The label "Made in The U.S.A." would no longer be appropriate. A shipping label on integrated circuits made by an

American company reads: "Made in one or more of the following countries: Korea, Hong Kong, Malaysia, Singapore, Taiwan, Mauritius, Thailand, Indonesia, Mexico, Philippines. The exact country of origin is unknown."

THE INDUSTRIAL POLICY BOARD could develop a market policy which would restrain companies from shifting operations abroad. The Board could make it more costly for companies to have products' components manufactured overseas.

There is no reason why domestic resources could not be used or developed to make the circuits described above. At its inception, this technology was created in the U.S. and shifted abroad to make things "easier" for the domestic producer.

The question of COST must be addressed. It is a reality that money can be made by manufacturing the circuits in the Philippines or one of the subsistence-wage Asian countries listed. Given a choice, and assuming that to make all the circuits in the U.S. would increase the cost of the product, the American consumer would be willing to pay a higher price for the end product if he could keep his $12 an hour job.

The American worker, having lost his job to the Philippine worker, now earns wages at $5 an hour versus $12 before being laid off. He cannot exist at this low $5 an hour wage, slips into poverty, and now joins the welfare community. This makes no sense at all in the terms of our national welfare.

The American worker, with reduced income, can no longer afford to buy the electronic product with the circuit board made in the Philippines. The electronic-maker now faces a shrinking market for his product. The bottom line is that, as the recession clearly indicates, the buying power of Americans will not meet the expectations of the retailer in our current economic decline. The casualty rate of Chapter 11 failures in the retail establishment is skyrocketing.

Personal bankruptcies number in the millions. Ironically, the trade deficit, covering imported products, also declines as consumers buy less.

TO OPERATE, LIVE, AND HAVE YOUR BUSINESS IN AMERICA MAY COST MORE, BUT YOU CAN ALSO TAP INTO A BROAD, PROSPEROUS CONSUMER MARKET IF THE JOBS FOR OUR WORKERS ARE IN AMERICA.

THE RECESSION IN THE U.S. THAT BEGAN SEVERAL YEARS AGO HAS SEEN A SHARP REDUCTION IN CONSUMER SPENDING, CREATING DOWNSIZING OF MANY MANUFACTURING FIRMS. A PUBLIC EARNING LOW WAGES OR UNEMPLOYED IS A WEAK MARKET FOR MANY OF THE PRODUCTS ONCE SOLD IN ENORMOUS QUANTITIES.

Germany: A Lesson That "Small In Business" Can Be Right

The Germans have long been famous for, and very proud of, what Germans call "Deutsche Qualität" (German Quality). Any product of "German Quality" is likely to be very good indeed. Year after year, small German plants grow in market size and are now the economic engine for Europe. The backbone of German industry rests in the hands of small companies with fewer than 500 employees.

These small companies produce 65 percent of Germany's gross national product, have an intensive apprenticeship training system, and in total employ about 75 percent of all the workers in Germany. It is reported some companies hire employees while they are still in high school and spend $18,000 a year for four years to train them as apprentices!

The small companies find a "niche" for their product and services. They think in global terms and plan to service the world. In their efforts, the German government gives ample financing, and the results have been outstanding. Germany today, because of its commitment to updating equipment and quality, is the largest exporter of textiles, greater than the Far East.

The assistance network, provided by their trade associations, bankers, and government, guarantees good results to the majority of exports centered around technology-intensive products.

American Small Business Can Revolutionize The Job Market

THE INDUSTRIAL POLICY BOARD could be the catalyst to further the role of small business in America. Our small business sector, completely ignored by our government, has for many years been the largest employer, paid more taxes than large companies, and created more new products than the large corporations in America.

Given the right economic climate, this sector could be the backbone of a new industrial revolution providing jobs and products for our sagging economy. These small companies have little voice in Washington, D.C., where the larger companies speak with loud voices and big campaign bucks for the Washington bureaucrats. There are signs of revolt, and small business is organizing its lobbying efforts to wring more consideration of its requirements from Congress.

It is from small business we can draw hope to reconstruct a stronger manufacturing base. In counseling clients at the Service Corps of Retired Executives, it is apparent to me that the young in America still have their dreams to start a business and "make it." These entrepreneurs need financial and counseling aid to establish effective business enterprises. A division of the *INDUSTRIAL POLICY BOARD* could structure the growth of this budding talent.

Immigration Must Be Controlled

Western Europe is alarmed over the migration of unemployed workers from the East European countries of Poland, Czechoslovakia, Yugoslavia, and Russia into Germany, France, Belgium, and Italy seeking work. The concerns are real. The numbers involved in this "invasion," as the West Europeans call it, have reached such proportions as to make it impossible for the host countries to absorb these people in the workplace and living space.

The measures now being planned by the Western European nations is to restrict this migration and plans are now under review.

The United States has for years been a safe haven for peoples from the four corners of the earth. When the economy is good, this immigration has been accepted. We are now in a different position. We have vast numbers of our people on welfare or living at the poverty level. The majority are not trained in the advanced skills required in the workplace.

The economic burden on American communities to absorb immigrants who will add to the enormous burden already carried by local and state governments dictates a change in immigration regulations.

We can no longer be the world's policeman, provider, and banker. The problem must be solved by the nations of the world working through the United Nations. Every nation would share in the responsibility of caring for others.

The disenchantment of Americans with Washington politicians is reaching a boiling point. The failure of elected officials to serve the interests of the public, and the crass greed of many members of Congress in "feathering their own nests," is resulting in a rejection of incumbents in office on a vast scale.

President Bush saw his popularity plummet to new lows when the economy did not improve as he and his advisors predicted. The millions of unemployed are fearful that our government does not have a plan to deal with our economic mess, and they are right.

Common Cause points out that political action committees (PACS) contributed $87 million toward House incumbents in the 1990 elections. Members of Congress are beholden to these financial supporters and have *insulated and isolated themselves from the public needs. Obsessed with power, they fail to recognize reality, and the country suffers. If there was some formula whereby nonperformers could be recalled, fired from office, it would be a great boon for the public.*

As to the future, politicians react and do not lead. An aroused public, such as we experienced during the Vietnam War, could effect change. We are moving in that direction.

The Creation Of An Industrial Policy Board Is Possible

The history of America records our ability to change when adversity overtakes us. We have few alternatives if we want to recapture some of our past industrial power. The proposal made in this book is not a fantasy but springs out of my experiences living in the dark days of The Great Depression and the recovery from that period.

There is a truth we have to accept. To live as we do as free people, with opportunities to use our talents in whatever fields they lie, demand that we pay a price for all these benefits. The price could be paying a little more for some products "Made In The U.S.A.," and perhaps it means accepting some products that may not be perfect. We can and must take this step.

If we give to our able-bodied people, willing to work, the security our forebears had, isn't it worth it?

INDEX

— A —

— B —

— D —

— E —

— F—

ABOUT THE AUTHOR

George Vargish was born in New York City and studied at New York University.

He spent fifty years in the Textile Industry, thirty-three years as the CEO of his own manufacturing firm, the Vargish Knitwear Co. For eight years, he was also President of Knitco Inc., his firm in Puerto Rico.

Mr. Vargish served as President of the National Knitwear & Sportwear Association from 1970 to 1980 and Chairman from 1980 to 1983. In addition, he was Chairman of the U.S. Apparel Council, representing the four largest Apparel Associations in the United States.

He served as an advisor to our government on bilateral trade agreements as they affected his industry and has frequently testified before Congressional Committees on trade issues.

Mr. Vargish is the author of *What's Made In The U.S.A.?*, a book dealing with the mismanagement of our trade affairs by our government. It was published by Transaction Books at Rutgers University.

His recent book, *Where Have All The Jobs Gone?*, published by Rainbow Books, Inc., addresses the economic distress of many Americans created by the lack of meaningful paying jobs. His new book offers a practical solution to our industrial problems.

Currently, George Vargish is lecturing on economic issues at various colleges and has been invited to present his views on TV and radio. He is a member of the International Advisory Board at Ramapo College and is a member of The International Trade Round Table at Bergen Community College.

He was a member of the American Arbitration Association, President of the Town Club, and three-term Mayor of Saddle River, New Jersey, where he presently makes his home with his wife.

Where Have All The Jobs Gone?

For additional copies of *Where Have All The Jobs Gone?*, telephone TOLL FREE 1-800-356-9315. MasterCard/VISA accepted.

To order *Where Have All The Jobs Gone?* directly from the publisher, send your check or money order for $14.95 plus $3.00 shipping and handling ($17.95 postpaid) to: Rainbow Books, Inc., Order Dept. 1-T, P.O. Box 430, Highland City, FL 33846-0430.

For QUANTITY PURCHASES, telephone Rainbow Books, Inc., (813) 648-4420 or write to Rainbow Books, Inc., P.O. Box 430, Highland City, FL 33846-0430.